The Journey of Unbecoming

The Journey of Unbecoming
Copyright © 2020 by Keba Richardson

ISBN- 13:9780578677637

Published by Pen 2 Pen Multimedia

This is an authorized biography. Names, locales, places, events, and people contained herein are purely from the author's memory, and/or from public record. This story is not intended to defame, intimidate, or ridicule any persons, living or dead.

$\mathscr{D}$edication

I dedicate this book first to my one and only sun... Tariq You have been my greatest source of inspiration and a constant reminder of what it means to love unconditionally.

Secondly, to my baby brother, Salih. Brother, I know who you are. I know how beautiful your mind and spirit is. I've always had your back and I still do. I have unwavering faith in you. You will find your way back to yourself. I love you to infinity.

Thank You For The love and support Keba

CONTENTS

∞
———— ⚬ ————

FOREWORD

By Doctah B Sirius

Caterpillars are born from butterflies with only one goal, to eat. They have no wings or reproductive organs. Day in and day out they crawl around eating every leaf they can find.

They are, in no way, aware of their future or past, and can only live in the now moment with no idea of what's to come of them. They are only aware of a voracious drive to consume as much food (information) as possible as quickly as they can.

Most end up being consumed by other animals helping to complete the life cycle of other animals. Many end up as fertilizer that helps the plants grow.

A very select few eat until they can eat no more then they begin to spin a cocoon, also known as a chrysalis, made of a crystallized silk; one of the strongest fibers on earth. It must be very strong to make it through the challenging winter months ahead.

Once inside the total darkness of this crystal cave, something amazing begins to unfold. You see, there are these small disk-like structures inside each caterpillar called imaginal cells. Only recently did scientists have any knowledge of these disk and their function.

Until this point in the caterpillar's life, these cells have been motionless floating near the genes, and now suddenly, they begin to activate, move around, link together, and create larger structures. At this point, the caterpillar's life force begins to wane, it is actually dying inside the crystal cave.

Even as its life is slipping away its old immune system (old habits), which in no way recognizes these foreign objects (new ideas), attacks them with the last of its life force.

This last attempt of the caterpillar to maintain its old life is futile and the life of the caterpillar slips away as its body turns into a soup. The imaginal cells gain more and more life force while using this caterpillar soup to create something new over the next few months.

The first thing the imaginal cells create are antennas that receive instructions from the cosmos as to the nature of the new being evolving now. This information joins with the imaginal cells to create wings for flight, adorned with beautiful colors with sacred geometric patterns, eyes that recognize the beauty of flowers, and a special body that is as light as a feather.

After months of development, the new being awakens one morning when the sun crosses the equator on the spring equinox.

This new being then produces the most powerful Enzymes known to man with the ability to eat through the crystal cave. Finally, after months in total darkness and harsh weather conditions, the new being is born as a butterfly. It stands on the edge of the cocoon, spreads it wings —it doesn't practice flying, it simply takes a big leap of faith and floats on air, up away never to return to its old life. It breaks free from the past. Its new life is one of grace, searching only for the most beautiful flowers to pollinate. It has gone through a most challenging life of metamorphosis, from the challenges of the caterpillar, to death inside the cocoon, to emerging as a beautiful butterfly bringing more life, love and peace to the world.

Scientists have recently found the caterpillar and the butterfly in no way have the same DNA; they are totally different beings. This is due to the alchemical nature of the imaginal cells and bio photons coming from the cosmos. They are so named imaginal cells because of their ability to seemingly be able to imagine a new life outcome.

It has also been realized that human beings also have imaginal cells that have the ability to create a new reality, a new outcome, a whole new life. To activate them one must be ready and willing to let go of what's been keeping them in caterpillar mode. Wise ones know this and do what must be done to create a metamorphosis in their lives, no matter how challenging it is.

When I met Keba, I saw the caterpillar, the cocoon, and the butterfly all at once, just as I do in most of my students.

I knew that if she had the will, the focus, the courage, and the fortitude that she would let go of who she thought she had become and emerge from her life challenges as someone totally new.

This book is about the ongoing journey that we all must undertake if we choose to rise and break free from the fears, habits, programs, curses, parasites, pirates, and challenges of our lives.

Are you ready to take the leap?

This is Keba's story, her Journey of Unbecoming who she thought she was, learning to fly while helping others do the same.

Are you ready?

Love, harmony, good health, and abundant wealth to you and yours.

Doctah B

ACKNOWLEDGMENTS

∞

First, I must thank the Creator of all things. Then, my parents for bringing an ambitious, fierce, focused, disciplined, woman into this world.

To my son, Tariq, you gave me a reason to go hard at a young age. You have been my greatest source of motivation.

To my oldest sister, Sabah, thank you for always believing in me, for all the ideas you listened to in the middle of the night, for calling me out on my shit when need be, and for being a great big sister.

To Doctah B Sirius, thank you for being a mentor, confidant, and friend. I am forever grateful for you and the wisdom you have selflessly shared with me.

To Cassie B., thank you for being a kind, trustworthy person. You are a great friend!

To Sedric, thank you for doing all my photography/videography, for believing in me and my vision from Day 1, and for being a kind, good-spirited person. You have helped me more than you know.

Thank you, Shaun Sinclair, for pulling me aside after

that presentation and helping me see the value in my story. Thank you so much for coaching me through this process.

Thank you to my siblings, family, friends, and acquaintances threaded throughout the book. You know who you are as you read it. Without you, there would be no story.

Thank you to all of supporters I have on social media who may not know me personally but share my content, repost my links, and engage with me daily. The love doesn't go unnoticed. I greatly appreciate you all!

INTRODUCTION

∞

Maybe the journey isn't so much about becoming anything. Maybe it's about Un-Becoming everything that isn't really you so you can be who you were meant to be in the first place -Paulo Coelho

As a young woman I was just like most people, led by the expectations and influences of everyone around me to the detriment of my own happiness. I was always smart, pretty, ambitious, and fearless, so I thought. I mean I had the degree, I had the money, I had the tall handsome husband, I'd popped bottles of Rose in $5000 VIP sections. I'd been on the shopping sprees, I'd possessed the designer bags, Gucci sneakers, and Jimmy Choo pumps. I'd flown business class to Brazil, and Africa, spent a week in Dubai, and vacationed on some of the most beautiful beaches in the world. You get the point... I lived and did everything "successful" people do.

Basically, everything that society says we should become, I became that *and* more, but during the hoopla of living my "best" life, I sustained an injury that grounded me — literally and figuratively.

During that time, I was forced to sit with myself and an epiphany came to me. I know it sounds cliché, but it's true.

Please believe I thought I was the shit. I was enjoying my life and I had no intentions on changing anything! But when the universe decides to call you, you have a choice to make. You either answer the call or ignore it. I chose to answer, although I didn't know it at the time.

Let me tell you how it happened...

It was the night after getting surgery on my fractured ankle. I was in my bathroom about to take my medicine when I looked at myself in the mirror and just broke down crying, which was very odd for me because I wasn't a "crier" or an emotional person at all.

Looking in the mirror that night I realized two things for the first time: 1) I was so fucking unhappy, and 2) I had no idea who I was.

I wasn't a religious or spiritual person at the time, but something told me to ask whoever was out there for guidance and clarity. I knew something had to change immediately because I couldn't stand to be the woman I'd been up until that point for another day.

After falling asleep that night something so bizarre happened. A voice came and literally woke me up! The voice said, "Now is time!"

I looked around my room like WTF; did that really happen??? I went back to sleep and all I can say is NOTHING was the same after I awoke the next morning.

"We delight in the beauty of the butterfly but rarely admit the changes it has gone through to achieve that beauty."

-Maya Angelou

That night began my journey of UN-BECOMING...

Un-becoming means breaking free from the matrix. In other words, freeing yourself from the expectations, cultural stereotypes, and opinions of what you thought you had to be and realizing you are the captain of your own ship in complete control of your destiny in life.

Un-becoming means doing a lot of un-learning and un-programming your mind. Then reprogramming your mind with true beliefs that serve you and your higher purpose.

Un-Becoming is understanding you are free to use your mind to manifest anything you desire in life.

Un-becoming means healing from emotional trauma, breaking free from generational curses, forgiving yourself for not knowing and creating a new narrative for your life.

Un-becoming means following your bliss no matter what.

Un-becoming is peeling back every layer until the only thing left is the real, authentic, highest version of you.

On my journey of un-becoming I became enamored with nature and learned to look to nature for answers to many of life's big questions. What's amazing is that nature gives us the perfect example of the journey of un-becoming through the Monarch butterfly.

The Monarch butterfly comes into this world as a small little speck of larvae. Once the larvae become a caterpillar, it's trying to eat what it can and do what needs to be done just to survive. The caterpillar has beautiful markings and is already destined to have wings and turn into a butterfly, but the caterpillar has no clue of its inherent destiny.

Just like so many of us as we're coming of age, we are in survival mode doing what we must do just to get by. We are all put here to serve a higher purpose and live a fulfilling life of abundance, but we are oblivious to our own inner beauty and inherent destiny, so we manage to survive by finding false happiness in things outside of ourselves.

xv

However there comes a time in a caterpillar's life where the inner butterfly demands it to become something more.

From there, the caterpillar spins itself into a chrysalis. While in the chrysalis, cells called *imaginal cells* kick in and the caterpillar turns into liquid goop, essentially *unbecoming* the caterpillar so it can be what it's meant to be — the butterfly!

Once the butterfly emerges from the chrysalis it takes a moment to inflate its wings. When the butterfly takes off it's now exactly what it's meant to be, and you'll never see that butterfly as a caterpillar again.

Unfortunately, less than 10% of caterpillars ever make it through this journey and become butterflies.

We are not so different from the Monarch butterfly. For us to be the highest, truest version of ourselves, we must UN-BECOME everything we thought we were also.

Just like the caterpillar there are only a select few of us willing to go through the journey of Un-becoming so we can find out who we really are.

For me, breaking my ankle and having to take a hard look at myself in the mirror was what prompted me to begin spinning my own chrysalis.

In this book I share with you the journey of a woman who came from a broken home plagued by mass incarceration, addiction, and dysfunction. A teenage mother, a former stripper, and woman who defied the odds to reach the pinnacle of "success".

This is the journey of a woman who became "Everything" only to "Un-become" it all.

If you are reading this right now, my highest hope is that this book will be the catalyst for you to begin spinning your own chrysalis so you can start your journey of UN-Becoming.

Welcome to the journey…

Part 1: Larvae (Childhood)

1

∞

How It All Started

My earliest traumatic childhood memory was the night my dad went to prison. Of course, I was too young to remember all the details, but I do know prior to that night my dad and I had an unbreakable bond.

I was my dad's first-born child and I was a super daddy's girl. I traveled with him to California and Tennessee, just the two of us. My mom said she would have to call his phone and bug him about bringing me back home. I looked so much like him when I was born, he said he screamed when he first saw me. He said friends would tell him, "*You're gonna have to ride around with a shotgun for her when she gets older.*" He would just laugh.

I remember my dad telling me about a trip we took once. He said I had my little carry-on bag rolling behind me as we walked through the airport, and once we got to our hotel in Memphis, I ate so many green grapes I got sick with diarrhea and shit everywhere. He had to put me in the shower and hose me down with the shower head.

He used to hide candy up on the top shelf in the kitchen and couldn't figure out for the life of him how I kept finding it. He said one night he hid behind the kitchen wall to watch me in action. He said I pulled a chair from the kitchen table up to the counter, then put my baby chair on top of the big chair, climbed on top of the counter, then climbed the shelves like spider man to get to the top shelf where the candy was. He said he couldn't believe how brilliant my tactic for finding the candy was... I was only two.

We went on trips to Disneyland. Me and my siblings wore the best clothes and shoes. Fur coats, Buster Brown shoes, Guess jeans and we even had a housekeeper who lived in-home with us. My dad would let us go in Toys R Us and get whatever we wanted.

My dad drove a red Porsche 944 Turbo, and a 7-series BMW with a phone in it — and that was just two of the *five* cars we had back then. In fact, the red Porsche 944 was his second Porsche. He told me he was driving down the interstate in Memphis one day and crashed his burgundy Porsche 924 Turbo. He left it at my great grandmother's house and went and bought the red Porsche 944 Turbo right off the showroom floor the same day.

My dad was fun, loving, and really enjoyed spending time with his family. My mom said he was mesmerizingly attractive in his youth. He wore clothes tailor made from the finest imported materials, Brioni suits, and owned a fully dressed Presidential Rolex that he bought off the arm of his jeweler in downtown LA. He shopped in Neiman Marcus and Saks Fifth. He had over 100 pairs of shoes from Certo in Beverly Hills. Certo made shoes for the stars, including Michael Jackson. However, his favorite pair of shoes were a pair of bespoke crocodile loafers he purchased from Bal Harbor in Miami for over $1000.

He dined at all the top restaurants in Beverly Hills. When he walked into a room his energy took over; he looked and smelled like money.

We lived in a nice home in Riverdale, Georgia, which back in the 80's was a very nice "white" suburban area to live in. Our home was furnished with top of the line contemporary furniture from a store in Buckhead, Atlanta called Huff. We had this glass case in our living room with a button on the side. When you pressed the button the entire top of the case lifted to reveal a TV inside. We had a black custom-made suede sectional that curved around the entire living room, a gold statue of King Tut, and a huge picture of the Great Sphinx on the wall.

My mom and dad vacationed in private villas in Jamaica and went horseback riding in Bermuda. My mom wore Gucci, Louis Vuitton, mink furs and she also had her clothes tailor made too. My dad provided my mom the funds to open her own nail salon. It was called *Just Nails*. Just Nails was the only upscale black owned nail salon in Atlanta. It was located off Old National highway, which in the 80's was a very prominent area for black people.

My mom had celebrity clientele like Evander Holyfield, Dominique Wilkins, the basketball wives, and all the big-time hustlers and their women. Her salon was so fly! The nail techs all wore white lab coats that said, *Just Nails*. They even had an in-house masseuse! My mom had her own nail polish and makeup line, and she was also going to New York to buy clothes to resale at the salon.

By now, you've probably guessed that my dad was in the streets. Yes, he was big-time, and he was at the top of the food chain in the world of coke. He and his crew were moving over 400 kilos a month. Simply put, he was a kingpin and we enjoyed the trappings of that lifestyle. However, you know the consequences of the "Life". It's only one or two options: 1) You die, or 2) You go to prison. Option number 2 came for my dad one night in November of 1987 as we were leaving my mom's nail salon.

I guess I forgot to mention that during this time of balling out and living in luxury my dad was a fugitive on the run for breaking out of prison some years prior for a different crime. He had a police chief on his ass and this man was obsessed with catching my dad. The chief told my dad he thought about him every morning when he had his coffee and he was determined to catch him before retiring. Unfortunately for us, the detective was pretty good at his job, and he did just that

Me, my little brother, my mom —who was 7 months pregnant with my youngest brother— and my dad had just left her nail salon. We were on the way to their favorite Indian restaurant, *Haveli*. My dad stopped at the gas station right by the salon and went in. My mom stayed in the car with us.

According to my mom, a few seconds after my dad went in the store, about 8 police cars pulled up and she said to herself, "Oh Fuck". She knew it was over, she knew they were there for my dad.

The police waited until my dad got back in the car and then surrounded the vehicle. They put him and my mom in cuffs then separated them. They put my mom in one car, my dad in another, and me and my brother in another. My mom said my brother was calm, but I was going bat shit crazy. She said I was kicking the officers and screaming and crying at the top of my lungs.

My mom said she couldn't really cry or process her emotions because they took her to the station and interrogated her for hours.

Our housekeeper came to the station to get me and my brother while my parents remained there for questioning.

My mom grew up in the Nation of Islam, so she was well aware of her rights. She knew she didn't have to answer any of the questions they asked her. The chief got in her face,

5

tried to intimidate her, tried to bribe her, and even called her a bitch, and she still wouldn't budge. So, they took her into custody, and she spent one night at Jefferson street jail.

After being released from jail she said the reality of my dad being gone hit her hard and she knew her life would never be the same.

As for me, at the young age of two, I lost my dad and experienced my first heartbreak.

After my dad went to prison life drastically changed for us. My mother had to pick up the pieces. She was only 29 years old with 4 children and one on the way.

2

∞

The Parentals

My mom was born in Watts, California and raised in the Crenshaw District. She graduated from Crenshaw High School. My dad was born in Memphis, Tennessee and raised in Inglewood California. He graduated from Morningside High School.

My parents initially met as teenagers in the Nation of Islam. My mom was a captain in charge of training new believers and my dad was in one of her orientation classes.

My mom was beautiful, with skin the color of honey, beautiful sandy brown hair, high cheekbones, and the brightest smile. Not to let her pretty looks fool you though, she was also militant, raw, and uncut. She'd grown up in the Black Panther Party and was a Crippette in the Crip gang out of Horace Man Jr. High. She was blunt and fearless.

My mom came from a family of 6: 3 boys and 3 girls. Her father was in and out of prison during her childhood, so she was raised by my grandmother and her stepfather, Boss Man, who was a professional boxing trainer. He used to train Muhammad Ali. He and my grandmother were in the Philippines for the Thrilla in Manilla.

Growing up, my mom said she always knew she wanted to have a lot of children and that she wanted to become a teacher. But that goal was a distant one being that she grew up in ground zero of the gang and drug epidemic in South Central Los Angeles.

She was surrounded by crack and heroin addicts and immersed in LA gang culture. My mom's brothers were friends with Tookie Williams. One of her childhood boyfriends was shot in the head and killed by a rival gang while on the way to her 15th birthday party, and her oldest brother was killed when she was 20. She'd seen and experienced a lot at a young age, so the Nation of Islam became her place of refuge.

My mom knew drugs and gang culture wasn't the right path for her she became a serious Muslim by the time she was 18 and the Nation was where she found her purpose. She became a top captain and top earner from selling bean pies. Nobody brought in more money than her.

In the 80's a group of top believers from the Nation moved to Atlanta to start the movement in the South. At the time my mom was "unhappily" married to my two older sisters' father.

Around the time my mom came South, my dad came South too because his family was originally from Memphis and he was between Tennessee and Georgia for work. My dad ended up catching a case in Dooley County, Georgia. He escaped from jail while awaiting trial for that case.

When my dad escaped from jail my mom was one of the first people he called for help. She agreed to help him and got him situated at a close friend's house. She would stop by throughout the week to check on him and bring him what he needed so he could lay low.

She and my dad previously had a thing for each other while in LA but never acted on it. By this time my mom and her husband were separated, and he was back in LA. With her and my dad spending so much time together, other sparks flew. My mom and dad ended up falling in love with each other.

Her husband came back a few months later and she attempted to reconcile with him, but she knew in her heart she wanted to be with my dad. I was conceived during this time. I was their secret love child, but her husband was under the belief I was his daughter too. The moment her husband saw me, he knew I wasn't his daughter. My mom ended up leaving him to marry my dad.

After marrying my dad, my mom had my first younger brother. She was pregnant with my youngest brother —her fifth child— when my father was captured and sentenced to 10 years in prison.

Before my dad went to prison my mom expanded her business and opened a second location a few miles away on Godby road. After he went to prison, she decided to close the Old National road location and keep the Godby road location because the rent and overhead was cheaper.

After a few years of my dad being incarcerated my mom decided to close her nail salon altogether. Being a full-time entrepreneur and single mother of five took its toll on her. She wanted to go back to school for something that would give her a more practical schedule like being a teacher. She decided to attend Georgia State University where she majored in middle childhood education.

Shortly after my mom enrolled in school, we had a huge fire in our home in Riverdale. As a result of the fire, we briefly moved to a smaller home while our house was being repaired. We eventually moved back to our home in Riverdale and that's where shit took a major left turn.

In the process of my mom closing her salon and going to school to become a middle school teacher, she met a new guy, a younger dude that I'll refer to as the "Evil Jamaican" and he quickly moved in with us too. My dad was still sending my mom money from prison until he found out about the Jamaican dude from a friend who stopped by to give my mom some money on my dad's behalf.

Side note: You know, it's scientifically proven that a child receives the majority of its programming during the ages of 0-7, and that this programming is the largest deciding factor on who most people become and how they handle situations throughout life.

Prior to the night my dad went to prison, his love was present. We had money, we lived well, and life was good. Abruptly that was taken away, and suddenly, the fatherly love was absent, and the money was gone, replaced with an evil stepdad and a narcissistic mother.

From my earliest memory until I was in the 6th grade, we lived in the home my father bought in Riverdale, it remained furnished with the furniture he bought, and even some of the bills remained in his name. At first, it was just the five of us. Then my mom had my two youngest sisters with the evil Jamaican. Me and my sister (who's 3 years older than I) shared a room upstairs on the right side of the house. We could see out front from our bedroom window. My oldest sister had her own room right next to ours until the two youngest were born. Then they all shared that room, and my brothers shared a room downstairs. The Porsches, Bimmers, and Benzes were gone. What we had left was the grey Chevy station wagon —the car the housekeeper used to drive us kids around in.

We called it the Wagon. It was ashy grey, and so old by now the lining on the ceiling hung down and you'd get little pieces of dust in your hair. The blinkers didn't work so my mom had to use hand signals, and after a while it started backfiring. We would all cram in. I can still hear my oldest sister yelling shotgun claiming the front seat before we all got in, until we changed the lingo and started saying Tec-9 instead of Shotgun. My mom was the queen of taking us to do fun free stuff. We'd go to the festivals at Piedmont Park, to the library, and she'd let us take turns going with her to school.

Because we had a nice home, we had clothes to wear, and food on the table, I didn't realize we were poor when I was a young child. I had no concept of that as my older sisters did. Because they were older during the years of living in luxury with my dad, they could see and feel the drastic difference.

We were on welfare. My mom would give us each a $1 food stamp before we'd go to the park so we could pick our own snacks and I thought that was the best thing ever. Meanwhile, my older sister who understood what food stamps were, would be upset and embarrassed about us having to use them because none of our other friends were on welfare.

We were that other kind of poor; we didn't go without the basics, but we didn't have what any of our other friends had. When I was young, Riverdale was a nice area where everyone came from two parent homes, where both parents were blue- or white-collar workers. All our friends had nice cars, wore nice clothes, had all the game systems and toys, they could afford extracurricular activities, and they had pantries full of food and we didn't.

My mom wasn't a huge disciplinarian when we were young. I never once got a spanking from her. She let the evil Jamaican handle that part. She just had an energy about her, and we knew we had to listen to her and respect how she ran her household.

She would take all of us to the grocery store with her and before getting out she'd give us the rundown: don't run, don't play, stay right with me, and don't put nothing in the cart. For the most part we always obeyed but if you did get

11

out of pocket while in the store, she'd give you the sharpest look. That look was enough to kill, and every now and then she'd pinch the shit out of you if that look wasn't enough.

My mom was very liberal. She didn't filter us from watching or listening to anything. She'd talk about real adult, inappropriate shit right while we were in the room. She cursed like a sailor, and she spoke her mind unapologetically. I can remember coming home from elementary school telling her something my teacher did that was unfair, and her response was: "That Bitch!!!!" That was one of her infamous sayings growing up.

My mom had 7 children by the time she was 35 and if you were to walk into our home, you'd never even know it. She ran a tight ship and we all had to contribute. We all had a night to cook, the older girls had a day to grocery shop, and we all rotated duties each week. We didn't call them chores, we called them duties. We knew the drill as soon as we got home from school too. It was to eat a snack, do homework, and do our duties before going outside.

Every Saturday morning the entire household got up early to clean everything from top to bottom. On Saturdays we did the real dirty work. The refrigerator/freezer got cleaned out completely, windows had to be washed, ceiling fans cleaned, and baseboards scrubbed. Our house was always immaculately clean. We ate dinner together as a family at the table every night, Sunday-Thursday. Friday and Saturday nights would be our junk nights. My mom would let us get frozen pizza chips, and ingredients for Root Beer Floats. On Sunday mornings, we'd eat a big breakfast together.

My mom was a black Muslim woman from the West coast and because of that we did things in our home way different from what our neighborhood friends did. For one, my mom was very open. She would walk around with her breast out like tribal women in Africa. She had no shame in being nude. I hated that!!! It drove me nuts and made me so uncomfortable as a child. We ate different too. We didn't eat pork, we didn't eat soul food, or drink Kool-Aid. We were eating enchiladas, LA style tacos with the fried tortillas, bean soup, candied carrots, and baked Cornish hens.

People thought we were weird because we ate turkey bacon and didn't eat pepperoni on our pizza. Also, because we ate a lot of meals that did not include meat before we even knew "vegan" was a word. The Jamaican also introduced us to Caribbean cuisine. Mangoes, plantains, and Johnny cakes were also things none of my other friends ate.

I lost one of my front teeth eating a mango seed and I lied and told my friends at school I was eating an apple because I knew damn well they didn't know what a mango was and I didn't want to have to explain.

I'd learned how to compartmentalize my friends at a young age. I knew how to make friends think they knew me or were close to me when they were not. I never really invited people into my home because I knew we were different, and I didn't want people to know about my dad. All my friends came from two parent homes, and none of them had family members in prison like I did. I only had one friend I would really say I was close to that I would invite over to my house to spend the night, and even she didn't know about my dad. It was too shameful and painful to explain to her, so I never brought him up.

I used to be so embarrassed in Elementary school when my mom would go in to let my teachers and the cafeteria staff know I needed an alternate tray because I didn't eat pork. After my dad went to prison my mom was no longer active in the Nation of Islam so I didn't really understand why we didn't eat certain things or why we didn't celebrate holidays other than Thanksgiving. To this day I'm not sure

13

why my mom made an exception for Thanksgiving. I will say, though, in our home we knew the truth about Thanksgiving. We knew what we were taught in school was B.S.

Because we did not celebrate traditional holidays, birthdays in my family were equivalent to Christmas. We went all out for birthdays. The whole living and dining room would be decorated with balloons and streamers. My mom would let us pick whatever we wanted to eat for our birthday dinner. I always chose crab legs and shrimp because to me that felt fancy.

We'd pile all our gifts in front of the glass case in the living room and open them one by one showing each gift off with such pride in our faces. We didn't sing the regular happy birthday song either; we sung the black version made up by radio host Ryan Cameron. Once that song came out it became the official birthday song in our household.

Barbies and books were always on the list of things I wanted for my birthday. *The Babysitters Club* books and the *Addy* books from the *American Girl* series were my favorites. I loved, loved, loved playing with dolls and all my dolls were black. My mom found black girls playing with white dolls to be utterly ridiculous. I would do their hair and drift off into my imagination with my barbies for hours at a time, living my life vicariously through them.

I played with dolls every single day which was odd because I was also a major tomboy. My mom would beg me to wear dresses and bobby socks, but I loved running and playing with the boys in my tennis shoes.

I was closest with my brothers growing up. We shared a special bond with each other. For one, the three of us had the same biological father. Also, because my dad had been the last man my mom was with (and they were still legally married) the evil Jamaican had a particular disdain for the three of us, especially my brothers. I always felt protective over my brothers when we were young. My mom also grouped us together and would call us by my father's last name as if we were some separate fucking entity from everyone else or something. I don't think she ever knew how much I hated that and how much it made us feel inferior when she did it.

She always treated us three different too, but it was much more noticeable with my brothers. So many times, she did things only for the older girls, other times she would do stuff for all the girls and leave my brothers completely out.

My stepdad would beat my brothers and punish them for weeks at a time for the dumbest shit. I used to hate hearing them screaming and crying downstairs. I would be in my bed upstairs thinking of all the ways I could kill that nigga. And it also began a deep-rooted disdain for my mother because I could not understand for the life of me how she could allow a man to be so mean to us, especially my little brothers.

My brothers were very hard sleepers and it took them forever to get up in the morning. I knew if they missed the bus they'd get a whooping and have to stay in their room for two weeks as if they were prisoners or some shit. So, I used to tell myself before going to bed each night that I had to get up an hour early.

I would get up extra early with no alarm clock so I could wake them up to get ready so they wouldn't get in trouble. They were my baby brothers; I hated seeing them in trouble. *And* we had a damn clubhouse to build so I needed them outside with me and the rest of our neighborhood crew.

My mom was a full-time student at GSU, and she worked too so she was gone all day while the evil Jamaican was home with us. I made it my business to stay out of dude's way. I used to pretend he didn't even exist. I never made eye contact with him, and I never initiated a conversation unless I had no other choice. If he was walking up the stairs, I'd go back down the hall until he was upstairs before I walked down. If my mom sent him to pick me up from anywhere there would be dead silence the entire ride between us. I despised him, I hated his guts, and had no words for him at all.

He had an explosive temper so we all tiptoed around him because the slightest thing would set him off. Everyone in our neighborhood feared him too.

He'd go off on loud rants speaking in patois. *Bombaclaat* this and *Rasclaat* that. *You wanna romp with me?* Then he'd normally throw or break something, storm out of the house, and leave for a while before coming back. That was his routine.

One night we were all at the table eating dinner. He got mad at my mom because he wasn't happy with what she cooked so he went off on one of his explosive rants and ripped the entire oven door off before storming out of the house. It was crazy! I never once recalled my mom arguing back with him when he went off. She'd just look at him like he was crazy. Every time he stormed out, I would hope and pray the nigga would never fucking come back.

Because we were home with the evil Jamaican while my mom was doing her thing, me and my brothers spent a lot of time playing outside. We had a huge wooded area in our backyard. We'd play in the woods all day. We were determined to build a clubhouse with our neighborhood friends. We'd gather sticks, leaves, and old paint, and everything we did was for the "clubhouse" that never actually got built.

We got into all kinds of shit outside too. We played, *Nigga Knock*. We made up this game called, *Hit the Deck*, where we'd hit the ground every time a car drove by and pretend we were dodging bullets. We used to vandalize vacant houses. We vandalized this one house so bad we broke all the mirrors, lit firecrackers in the toilets, and plastered a bottle of rotten BBQ sauce we found in the cabinets all over the house. We felt bad and tried to go back the next day to clean it up some, but the damage was done.

When it was raining, we played inside. We had a den downstairs in our house. We could close the den door and play. The evil Jamaican didn't normally come down there to bother us. Because I had so many siblings, and because my mom always left our door open to family members in need, someone always lived with us. An aunt, uncle, cousin, or family friend; it was never a dull moment.

We would play hide and go seek in the dark. Then we would turn the entire downstairs into a huge tent. We even played news once, like, we literally made a news set, had a crew, news copy and everything! But our favorite game ever to play was a game we made up called, *Comedy*.

One person had to stand up and do funny stuff and everyone else had to refrain from laughing or else they'd have to get up in front of everyone next. I was a master at holding my laughs in because I was super shy, and I didn't want to have to get up in front to make everyone else laugh. We had a saying before the game got started: *"No laughing, no speaking, no showing your teeth. If you're the monkey, the monkey may speak."*

I don't know where that saying came from but it was game on after that was said, and if you so much as showed your teeth, you were out. Damn, we had fun playing that game!

Except for the evil Jamaican, life in Riverdale as a young kid was cool. We lived in a great neighborhood with plenty of friends. I had so much fun playing outside, racing, having water gun fights, and walking to the candy lady's house for hot fries and grape soda. But inside of the home, things were about to shift majorly for my family.

Prior to the summer before my third-grade year, I was a green little girl who'd grown up in a middle-class suburban area. Yeah, we were technically poor. We didn't wear name brand clothes, we shopped at outlet stores, my mom got our clothes on layaway, we didn't have cable, and we were on welfare. One time, we went a whole year without having a phone but honestly, I didn't know we were poor.

I never saw or heard about violence in our community, and overall, it was a nice place to grow up. I didn't know anything about the hood, I'd never been to the projects, I'd never went without lights or hot water, I didn't know gangs were a real thing, and I'd never seen any type of street violence in my life.

The summer before my third-grade year of school, me and my two older sisters flew to Los Angeles with my mom's mother who we all called Grandmommy. We were going to spend the entire summer there with her and our cousins.

3

∞

California Dream Turned Nightmare

I remember being so excited walking through the airport. Back then there was no TSA; my mom walked with us onto the plane and stayed on as long as she could until it was time for us to take off. When we got to California, we went to the townhome my Grandmother shared with my uncle and two cousins in Bellflower, which is about 25 minutes from LA. It was beautiful! The townhome was modern, exceptionally clean, and decorated very nicely. Reconnecting with my cousins was nice too. Although I didn't remember them, I felt an immediate closeness to them, and we were thick as thieves that entire summer —we had to be.

After the first few weeks of being in California shit got real. My grandmother was a strict Muslim. She didn't eat meat at all, she didn't eat fast food, she didn't eat anywhere with devils cooking in the back either. (She referred to all white people as devils.) According to her, EVERYTHING had pork in it so we couldn't eat candy, gum, fruit snacks, or pizza. My grandmother had us drinking carrot juice, eating falafel, and ordering veggie burgers from Simply Wholesome.

One afternoon my older cousins got the bright idea to sneak and order pizza while Grandmommy was gone. When the pizza came everyone ate lightning fast and ran upstairs. I was the youngest, I ate the slowest, and right as I was finishing my last slice she walked in and yelled, "KEBA!!! What's that in your hand????"

I was almost shaking in my pants when I turned around and said, "Pizza."

She went the fuck off, washed all the dishes in bleach, and lectured us all.

Grandmommy was very much rooted in Islam and she lectured us it seemed like every day for 3-4 hours at a time about knowledge of self, our history, the white man, and why we couldn't trust Devils.

She told us a story about being in a department store as a young girl in Oklahoma City and how this little white girl followed her around the store the entire time she was there calling her a nigger. Her disdain for white people was very confusing for my young mind because I had not been taught to hate white people. I had white friends at school, my girl scout troop leader back home was white, and it was very hard for me to imagine all white people being Devils... but my grandmother was stern and unwavering about her opinion back then. So, I learned a certain level of hate for Devils that summer, especially the police. They were the worst Devils of them all, according to my grandmother.

We had to leave the house each day by noon and stay gone until after 6. And man did we get into some shit between 12-6! There were 5 girls with me being the youngest. We had two bikes and a scooter to get around on and no money in our pockets. I was always on the handlebars of one of the bikes and we rode out on those bikes day in and day out. We'd go to the corner store and hit them for all our favorite snacks. I had Lucas, Saladitos, and turkey jerky for the first time on one of our stealing sprees. We'd go to my oldest cousin's boyfriend's house sometimes but mostly we went to the park around the corner.

One of my cousins was a super-duper tomboy and she was very influenced by LA gang culture. We were at the park one day and she said, "Keba you see that girl right there?"

I said, "Yeah."

She said, "I don't like her; go slap her."

I didn't even think twice. I walked right up to this girl who was much bigger than me. I was 7 years old going on 8 and she was 11 years old. I tapped her on the shoulder and when she turned around, I said, "BITCH!!!!" and slapped the shit out of her. I walked away while she just stood there crying with the whole side of her face blood red. They later nicknamed me B.G. —Baby Gangster!

I was exposed to so much that summer in Cali. I had never stolen anything in my life but became a pro at stealing from the corner store. I'd never heard West coast rap but quickly learned every single word to Ice Cube's, "Today was a Good Day." I'd never seen gangbangers in my life but quickly learned about colors.

So much went down at that park around the corner. I watched my cousin get jumped into a gang. I just stood there watching her get beat up by ten other girls, not knowing what to think. Then weird stuff started happening. We were being harassed by random police officers and followed by unmarked cars. One day we were at the park and this officer came over and pretended to dig something out of the trash. He held up a random ass fingernail file that came from who-knows-where and accused my oldest cousin of tagging on the table with it. We all looked at each other in amazement like, *is this cop serious?* He tried to arrest my cousin and she

21

ran. He eventually caught her, put her in cuffs, and drove us home. I couldn't believe that officer arrested my cousin for no reason. My grandmother was right about Devils. I didn't understand what was going on or know what to think until the first night the bounty hunters busted into the townhome. They fucked the whole house up, ransacked everything, knocking over hampers, pulling everything from the closets, snatching down the shower curtains and everything looking for my uncle who I found out that night was a fugitive from justice... a big-time fugitive.

My grandmother was so pissed when she got home. She lectured us for hours about what was going on, what we needed to look out for, and how we needed to move going forward.

Everything went downhill for the summer after that. We were harassed and followed daily, the bounty hunters would purposely wait until they knew my grandmother wasn't home to bust in and ransack the house. Our lights and hot water got cut off, not for nonpayment, but because we were being harassed. We had to boil water to bathe, wash our clothes in the tub, and light the stove with matches to cook.

The townhome got too hot. Police officers, bounty hunters, and detectives were lurking everywhere; it was too much so eventually we all had to leave.

From there we shuffled from sleazebag hotel to hotel in Compton for a few weeks before my grandmother sent us all to Riverside to stay with another uncle of ours and his wife for the remainder of the summer.

Man, Riverside was a trip! It felt like we were in the middle of no fuckin where. I had never been in a house with no food at all until being at my uncles. Like the cabinets, the refrigerator, and freezer were empty. There were ten of us in a 2-bedroom house. We were walking to the grocery store to steal food to cook. My uncle and his wife fought every single day nonstop. It was the craziest shit I'd ever seen. Then they somehow got a hookup on Little Caesars pizza and we ate foot long pizzas with cheese and pineapples every day. So much so I started hating pizza, but I did appreciate them putting us on cheese pizza with pineapples on top though. We took that one back home to Riverdale with us.

Summer was over and it was time to go back home. With everything going on my grandmother had gotten short on money and used what my mom sent for our plane tickets back on bills. So, me, my sisters, my grandmother, and my cousin (whose father was on the run) rode the Greyhound for 4 gruesome days from Cali to GA.

The bus ride was the worst experience ever. We didn't have seats together for a lot of the trip. I remember this obese white woman laying on the floor in the back of the bus coughing up blood. Her feet kept touching my sisters' stuff and I was pissed about it. I kept tugging on my sister letting her know the woman's feet was touching her stuff, but I don't think my sister was as bothered by it as I was.

We got off in Oklahoma City to get food and the bus left us. My grandmother chased that bus down beating on the side. The bus eventually stopped and let us get on. We arrived at the bus station in downtown Atlanta a few days later.

Overall things were different for me and my family after that summer. For one, I was no longer the green 7-year-old I was prior to going. Two, the drama with my uncle who had by now become one of America's Most Wanted followed us back to the suburbs.

On my brother's 7th birthday, we were having a great time as we always did with birthdays in our house when all of a sudden the house was flooded with bounty hunters and cops going through the house just as they did in Bellflower. They were looking for my uncle.

An episode of *Georgia's Most Wanted* aired shortly after that with my uncle's story and description. A lot of our neighbors and childhood friends saw that and we felt it. Some of our neighbors stopped speaking to us altogether. Other neighbors told my mom the police had visited their homes and asked for their cooperation in capturing my uncle.

A short while after his story aired on *Georgia's Most Wanted,* my uncle was captured and sentenced to Life in prison —Fed Time. His daughter, who was 3 years older than me, moved in with us after he caught his time and she became just like a sister.

Her living with us was cool. She was one of my favorite cousins. She and my older sister were the same age and had a tight bond. They did everything together.

A few years later the evil Jamaican's daughter moved in too. She was super slim and freakishly tall, at least 6'3". I'd never seen a girl that tall in my life. Everywhere we went people would just stare at her. I never felt embarrassed being with her though. She was sweet, and I enjoyed having her there. I used to like doing her hair in the downstairs bathroom., she and I became very close. Her mom died when she was little, and she'd lived a hard life before moving with us. So, I felt sorry for her in a lot of ways.

So, we had a full house as usual. Because we were used to people staying with us it didn't cause any real shift in our household dynamic so things were as normal as they could be, considering the circumstances. However, by now my mom was only tolerating the evil Jamaican, and what he didn't know was she was plotting on a masterplan for us to move away from him.

Prior to the summer before my sixth-grade year I didn't know my dad's side of the family at all. We hadn't seen or been in contact with them since I was a baby.

Honestly my mom never really mentioned our dad or his family at all. She never once sat me and my brothers down and talked to us about him, or what he was like. I didn't even know my dad's middle name. I literally knew nothing about him. I would just piece together what I thought he was like in my mind from the photo albums we had. My mom decided to stop taking me and my brothers to see our dad when I was around 7 years old and I couldn't stand her for that.

I know it had something to do with her getting mad about seeing one of my dad's girlfriends at the prison, and him having her pink lipstick on his collar. I thought she was crazy for being mad. She had an evil Jamaican nigga living in the house my father bought and furnished, and she had already had one of my little sisters by this time too, so I felt her reasoning behind no longer taking us was pretty fucked up.

A friend of the family would come a few times a year to take me and my brothers to see him and my dad always wrote letters. He always had the best cards made for us for our birthdays and he had us enrolled in all sorts of programs for children with fathers in prison. So, we would get clothes and toys on holidays and special occasions through these programs.

Every time we went to visit, my dad was always in such good spirits. He was always laughing, making jokes, and very loving toward us. We would take turns sitting by him and on his lap in the visiting room, and we would buy a shit load of snacks from the vending machines. I would always feel so sad every time we left dreading the ride back home.

My dad's mother, whom we called Nanny, and my aunties sent for me and my brothers to come to LA for the summer. I had a totally different experience this time. It was nothing like the summer in Bellflower. Rather, it was a summer of carefree fun.

Nanny and one of my aunts stayed off Crenshaw and 78th street and my other aunt stayed off Crenshaw and 75th. All summer we took turns running back and forth spending the night between my Nanny's house and my aunt's house.

I can still hear Too Short's "Gettin It," Tupac's "2 of Amerikkkaz Most Wanted", and Bone Thugs's, "Meet me at the Crossroads" playing in my head. That's all we listened to that summer until I introduced my cousins to Kilo Ali and Raheem the Dream!

We had so much fun that summer, getting to know my dad's family, meeting so many cousins our same age, going to Venice beach, and going to the swap meet. We even took a road trip to Vegas which felt like a dream come true.

Vegas was magical! We stayed at The Stardust. I can still remember being in awe of the lights and how beautiful Vegas was at night.

We went to the Circus Circus Adventuredome, visited the volcano at the Mirage, and the pirate show at Treasure Island. We went to the Luxor and it reminded me of the gold statue we had of King Tut and the picture we had on our living room wall of The Great Sphinx back home.

My dad had about 2 ½ years left before he'd be released from prison and going to LA that summer made me more anxious and excited about him coming home. We'd gotten to see his childhood pictures, meet his side of the family, and see more of what he was like, so I felt more of a closeness to him.

4

∞

New Beginnings

Shortly after returning from LA that summer my mom was able to fulfil her dream of becoming a middle school Algebra teacher. After a year of working full time as a teacher she left the evil Jamaican and we moved to a 5-bedroom home in Morrow, GA.

Being in Morrow at that time was like culture shock. Before leaving Riverdale our neighborhood and that entire area had become predominantly black. When we moved to Morrow, we were 1 of 2 black families in our whole neighborhood. We had zero friends. In fact, my brothers would still get dropped off in our old neighborhood on weekends so they could hang with our old friends.

The culture shock wasn't just from our new environment, it was also the new dynamic in our household.

Before the move we were all close, especially me and my brothers and we had so many neighborhood friends. I'd always shared a room with my sister, and we did a lot as siblings with each other, but when we moved because of how we were split in age, the older girls had the big room downstairs. My two brothers shared a room, my two little sisters shared a room, and for the first time, I had my very own bedroom.

After moving I really started seeing things in my mom that I was too young to notice or comprehend before and it wasn't good. For lack of a better word, I despised her for several different reasons, but I was happy about having my own room.

My room was the size of a matchbox, but I loved it. I turned it into my sanctuary. I painted the walls bright yellow. I put posters of my favorite artists up, which back then was Usher, MA$E, and Dru-Hill. I put glow in the dark stars all over the ceiling and walls, so at night it was like I was in my own universe. Eventually, I even put a lock on the door that required a key for entry. It was really my sacred space and I didn't want anyone in there if I wasn't home.

I found myself spending a lot of time alone in my room, just thinking. I started analyzing my life and the role my mother played in it and I really started piecing together why I resented her so much. She allowed a man to move into my father's house and treat us (especially my brothers) like shit. She treated all her children noticeably different, and she always put herself first before her kids.

She would do things like not pick up the phone even if she was sitting right next to it, knowing it was one of her children calling. She would deny us rides home after school, or not pick us up after the movies, even if she was home doing nothing. If we participated in any extracurricular activity she was not going to pay. We had to be able to do it for free and we couldn't count on her to ever pick us up from practice. No exaggeration, she wouldn't take us to or from our games. Like, she only did what she felt like doing for us, and suddenly, I had nothing but anger and rage toward her.

At this time, I felt very misunderstood and alone although I never verbally expressed it. I was never an emotional person, and I was always very private about my feelings, so I would write out my frustrations and what I was feeling in my mind on notebook paper. I'd read it a few times then tear it up into little pieces.

My biggest fear back then was someone finding my innermost thoughts, so I always tore the paper up after.

By now I was too old to run and play with my brothers. Once my period started that was the end of my tomboy days, and I was too young to relate to my older sisters.

After the age of about 7, I was never close to my mom. I didn't go to her when I was upset or feeling sad like my other siblings did. I didn't lay in the bed with her or have a tight affectionate bond with her like my other siblings did.

I felt like I couldn't talk to anyone. I was at a new school, so I hadn't made many friends. A lot of people knew me because I was a new face and I was always popular in school. I had always been a very shy person but for some reason, my whole life, people just always naturally gravitated towards me. At this school, people really gravitated toward me because my mom let me get my nose pierced prior to starting school that year. So, I was known as the new girl with the earring in her nose. A nose ring back then was taboo; no one else had one. I'd only been able to convince my mom because both my grandmother and aunt had nose rings and it was more of a custom as opposed to a trend.

I wasn't a girly girl, but I was much more into my appearance and how I dressed. Unfortunately, money was tighter than ever. My mom literally depended on my sisters, who were in high school, to help pay bills.

I was no longer 7 years old now. I could see and feel that we were poor. Being in middle school, I cared about name brand clothes and the latest shoes and my mom just couldn't afford to get us what we wanted.

29

We didn't have cable, and our AC didn't work. The house would be stifling hot in the summer, and we barely had enough food to eat. I should've been grateful for having a roof over my head and a bed to sleep in, but I wasn't. I wanted to wear Jordans, rock Tommy Hilfiger, Nautica, and Polo, and watch BET afterschool like the other kids my age.

My mom decided to go back to school to get her Master's in education and when she graduated a lot of our family came from out of state for her graduation from GSU, including her father.

Everyone called him Pops. I didn't know him at all; he'd been in and out of prison for all my mom's life. All I'd heard were the crazy stories. I knew he'd been shot in both of his legs for trying to escape from prison and that he'd been a notorious criminal. I quickly learned he was off his rocker though because the first night he came to our house he refused to sleep inside, opting to sleep outside in a sleeping bag instead.

In fact, he never once slept in the house in the 10-plus years he ended up staying with us. Instead, he converted our back shed into what he called his "Retreat". Imagine a toolshed being turned into a studio. He had a bed, electricity so there was heat. He could make his coffee back there, and he had a TV. He was Tesla or Einstein genius; he knew so much about math and science he could fix anything, but he also was crazy than a muthafucka.

The first few months of him being there was cool. He was a great cook, he had a lot of funny stories, and I remember him saying if you go to college you should major in business. As time went on it was just something about him I didn't fuck with, but I couldn't quite put my finger on it. I began treating him much like the evil Jamaican, not really communicating with him unless I had to.

One day I was in the kitchen pouring a bowl of cereal and he asked me, "Keba why do you hate me so much?"

I just looked at him, shrugged my shoulders, and walked off.

One night, me, my two brothers, my cousin, and little sister got the bright idea to go nigga knocking. We thought it would be funny to knock on the retreat door and run. Me and my little sister didn't even go back and knock; we were just a part of planning it out. Pops didn't find my brothers and cousin nigga knocking on his retreat door to be funny. He thought it was disrespectful. He walked up from the back shed and slapped all of us dead in the face for playing with him.

And. I. Went. The. Fuck. Off.

My temper was very explosive, I wasn't scared to go off on anyone. I would cuss anybody out! Teachers, cashiers, old people… it didn't matter. If I felt disrespected, I was letting it be known.

So, he went upstairs to tell my mom what happened, and I went upstairs too. I was beyond furious!!! I was never a crier, but I was that so-mad-you-cry mad. I cussed him out right in front of my mom and told him to never say shit to me or touch me again. My mom was begging me to stop as if she feared what he might do to me.

I roared, "I'm not scared of that Old Ass Fool!"

He lunged as if he was going to hit me. By this time everyone was in my mom's room trying to diffuse the situation.

Later that night he told my brothers and cousin that if he had his gun on him, he would've killed them for knocking on his door and running.

Years later, we found out he was a pedophile from other members in our family.

31

Between my 7th and 12th grade year, we had an average of 13 people living in our house. In addition to Pops, there was my aunt, older cousins, younger cousins, and one of my uncles from LA that came to live with us. The house was more crowded than ever! Dinner time was like survival of the fittest. When you heard someone screaming, "EVERYBODY COME AND EAT!" from the kitchen at dinner time, if you were not at the table within 5 minutes you might not have a plate.

My mom was a middle school teacher and the head of household for 13 people, and we were constantly reminded of how tight her budget was. When I was in middle school my mom broke the news to me that she would no longer be buying my school clothes. After that, she literally never gave me money for anything related to school again for the rest of the time I was in school.

My disdain for my mother was bubbling over because I knew she could have bought me school clothes, but she was always concerned more with men, taking her staycations at hotels, and doing shit exclusively for herself. Like the time we were in the house starving and she was making a T-bone steak and baked potato for the married man she was in a relationship with.

One year she made me and my brothers choose between going on a beach vacation with her and my sisters or getting school clothes. Like, what kind of shit is that??? Why are you taking a vacation in the first place if you can't afford to buy all your children what they need for school? So, guess what? Me and brothers stayed home while they all went to the beach for a week. We got $75 each for school clothes. And she really wondered why I had no respect for her and why my attitude toward her was so bad?

Then, for her to have the nerve to tell someone that's NOT old enough to get a job, she can't buy them what they need for school without giving me any real notice was a deal breaker. There was no coming back from that. I had a permanent disgust for her, everything she said went in one ear and out the other. My mom inspired me in one way and one way only —and that was to be nothing like her.

I learned at a very young age that I could not depend on her, so I asked very little of her and kept my distance from her. I was like the black sheep of my siblings when it came to my mom. I was always mean, and I always had an attitude, and this situation with her telling me she was no longer buying me school clothes made matters worse.

Being who I was, I had to figure out something. I came up with a plan and used my older cousin's name and social and got a job at Arby's so I could buy school clothes.

The job at Arby's didn't last long, so I came up with other ways to get what I wanted. Me and one of my best childhood friends that I cheered with would put on our uniforms and go fundraising. We would keep all the money so we could get our nails done and buy school clothes.

One year, me and her got caught stealing clothes from the mall during Christmas break. We didn't want to be the only ones going back to school after the holiday without new clothes, so we went on a stealing spree. She'd been one of my closest friends since elementary and that wasn't our first time getting into some shit together. When we were in 5th grade, we took her mom's car for a joyride. We waited until her mom was asleep and she took the keys. The plan was for her to drive first, then I'd drive.

The car was parallel parked and when she put it in drive... BOOM! She hit the car in front of us. Then she put it in reverse and... BOOM! She hit the car behind us. I was laughing so hard I was peeing on myself. Once the car was out of the parking spot, we took turns driving around her apartments. Then we went and picked up two friends on the other side of the apartments and let them drive.

After that, the car broke down and we had to push it into a parking spot down the street from my friend's house. Her mom woke up the next morning freaking out. She thought someone stole the car. We confessed that we took it, drove it, and left it down the street after it broke down.

My friend was mixed — her mom was white and her dad was black, and I swear this girl could do anything and she never got in real trouble. After taking the car, all her mom did was tell me I had to go home. I was back over a few days later per usual. She lived in some hood apartments by the airport. I didn't even know it was the hood when I was a kid, I just loved going over there because there were so many kids and because their swimming pool was 9 feet deep.

During the summer we would stay in the pool all day and night. One day we were playing sharks and minnows in the deep end of the pool. This girl who was much bigger than me kept pulling me down in the water damn near drowning me so she wouldn't get caught.

After she did it about 3 times too many, I said, "Look, if you do that shit again Imma beat yo ass!"

I wasn't one to start stuff, but I was never scared of anyone and I always knew how to stand up for myself.

We all continued playing with no problem. When we got to my friend's house later that night, she said, "I bet you won't go beat ol' girl ass for trying to drown you in the pool earlier."

I said, "I bet I will."

We walked over to her door. My friend knocked and told her to come outside. As soon as she came out, I hauled off and hit her in the face. I knew I had to hit her big ass first if I wanted to win.

Once we moved to Morrow me and my best friend were on different sides of town and it got harder for us to hang out, so she and I eventually grew apart. During that time my older sisters and cousins had developed their own bond. They all hung out together. I was too young back then to vibe with them. My brothers were tight, and they had their crew of new neighborhood friends, and my little sisters were thick as thieves with each other and their neighborhood friends. I had 1-2 people I considered friends but didn't really feel close to anybody. So, I spent a lot of time in my room listening to the radio.

My favorite songs were, Lathun's, "Freak It", Usher's "You Make Me Wanna", KP & Envy's, "Shawty Swing My Way", and Chris Luva Luva's, "Phat Rabbit."

I would spend hours listening to music going through the high-end magazines such as *Vogue, Harper's Bazaar, W,* and *Architectural Digest* that my mom was subscribed to. I'd live a life of luxury vicariously through the pages. From a very young age I knew I wanted to be extremely wealthy, I would flip through the magazines and pick out my dream homes, furniture, clothing, and cars.

***

After living in Morrow for a while my dad was released from prison. When he came home, he was nothing at all like I'd expected him to be. I'd romanticized this version of what he'd be like when he came home in my mind. I envisioned this loving, caring, nurturing father. I created this dream home me, him and my brothers would live in, and an entire dream life we'd live with him far away from my mom. But that wasn't the case. Instead, he was pushy, impatient, brash, and could have an explosive temper. I quickly learned that, to my dad, money was more important than everything and

35

getting back on top was his Number 1 priority, not being a loving nurturing father.

Although I didn't get the fatherly love I expected, I learned my dad's way of showing love was through spoiling us with material possessions. He spoiled me and my brothers but because I was the only girl, he spoiled me to the maxxxx!

He'd pull up, beep the horn, and we knew it was time to eat good and hit the mall. I remember getting my first pair of Jordans that year to go back to school in after Christmas. For the first time ever, we went to the mall and got name brand clothes.

My dad was a trip. Me and my brothers had so many inside jokes about him, his mannerisms, and his expressions. He loved driving around looking at houses and new construction sites. He was very knowledgeable about money and business, but damn he was a know-it- all. You couldn't correct him about anything, and he listened to rap, which my mom wasn't too fond of, so I enjoyed riding with him.

That summer me, my dad, and brothers went on a cross country road trip. We drove from Georgia to California, making stops to visit family in Memphis and Las Vegas before reaching our destination of Los Angeles. We were in a red Jeep Grand Cherokee. I had the front seat and my brothers were in the back. We had a cooler full of snacks and drinks packed and we hit the road. I was super excited; this would be my third summer in a row going to LA. I couldn't wait to see my cousins and I was excited about the family I would be meeting in Memphis too.

This would be my dad's first time having the three of us by himself for an extended period and I don't think he was mentally prepared for three pre-teens on a road trip cross country.

We made it to Memphis and stayed with one of our uncles. He had a big house with a pool and the pool had a

diving board and slide. So, me and my brothers wd
all day and night. We met our great Grandfather. He still
lived in the same house my dad's mother was raised in. We
met cousins our same age that we never knew before, we
went to the circus, rode go karts, and had a great time overall
in Memphis. After leaving Memphis we hit the road and the
plan was to drive until we got to New Mexico.

Me and my brothers were all silly but my brother right
under me was a straight clown. He joked about everything,
and him and my youngest brother had developed their own
slang they would use with each other. It was funny as shit,
but my dad could not take it. He was so annoyed; he didn't
have the patience to deal with how silly and stupid we could
get.

My dad finally got fed up and screamed for everyone to
be quiet. We looked at him like, *yeah whatever*, and kept
laughing.

Then he said to us, "I swear if one person says another
word, I'm pulling this truck over and taking my belt off."

Right after he said it my brother made a joke and all
three of us died laughing. My dad quickly pulled the truck
over. Before he could get his belt off, my brother hopped out
of the truck and took off running.

We were literally in the middle of nowhere. My brother
was running through fields where cows were grazing. So, I
hopped out of the front seat to protect my brother from my
dad. I blanked out and went in full beast mode. I'm talking
to my dad like he's a nigga on the street.

"Fuck that, I don't give a fuck who you are! We don't
even know you like that; you ain't bout to whoop my
brother!" I yelled.

I'm running trying to catch up with my brother. Mind
you, I have on pajama shorts and a t-shirt. My legs were
getting welts on them from running through the cow fields.

I saw my dad go back to the truck. He said something to my youngest brother who was standing outside of the truck too by now. Then, he left my brother standing there and drove off. My brother finally stopped running through the cow fields and we met back up where our youngest brother was standing on the side of the road.

I said, "Where did he go? What did he say?"

My brother said, "He said 'come on let's go, we're leaving them.'"

My youngest brother's response was, "I'm staying right here with my sister and my brother."

We did not play about each other at all. My dad circled back, and we piled back in the truck, but instead of getting in the front this time, I rode in the back with my brothers until we got to Las Vegas.

My dad ended up apologizing to us. He felt bad, he knew he was out of pocket, and he honored the way we stood up for each other. We didn't experience anymore hiccups and it turned out being my most fun summer visit ever to LA!

I had an older sister from my dad I'd never met before. So, I spent most of the summer in Corona, California with her and we had a freaking ball, going to the mall, going to the teen club, and being fast, kissing boys. I tried smoking weed for the first time but didn't know what the hell I was doing so I never actually got high.

After being in Corona, the remainder of the summer was spent in Vegas before driving back home.

5

∞

BALLIN'!

By the time I was in high school my dad was back BALLIN'.

My dad would take me and my brothers to Lenox and Phipps to shop. Parisian at Phipps was one of my favorite stores back then. They would have apparel you couldn't find at Macy's and I liked having clothes I knew no one else would have. No one else at my high school was shopping at Phipps or Lenox like that. I remember wearing a BeBe outfit to school one day and someone asking me what that was, so I switched up a bit and Tommy Hilfiger became my favorite. I wore Tommy Girl and Air Maxes just about every day. I remember begging my dad for a pair of Prada sneakers and him saying I was too young and not ready for that yet.

When my dad stepped into stores like Gucci, they knew him by name. My dad was wearing Bally, Ferragamo, and smoking Presidential Kush way before I ever heard mention of it in a rap song.

One time, for Spring Break my dad got a double suite for me, him, and my brothers to stay in for the week. It was right across the street from Lenox. One morning we wanted room service. He told us we could order it. When the food came, the bill was over $200! We thought we were going to get in trouble. My mom would've killed us for even thinking about ordering room service, but that $200 was nothing to my dad. He didn't care at all. We hit the mall every day that week. I'd get 2-3 pairs of shoes at a time. I had over 10 pairs of Tommy Hilfiger jeans, and enough shirts to wear a different one for over a month without repeating.

We always ate good with my dad too. Benihana, Pappadeaux, and Houston's were like fast-food restaurants for him. To us, it was amazing! We had never eaten at fancy restaurants in Buckhead before. My mom did her best. From time to time, we would all go to IHOP for breakfast, Old Country Buffet for dinner, or a restaurant, but we could never order drinks with our food and we normally had to order appetizers only at restaurants. So, for the first time we could order anything we wanted.

My dad would say, "Daughter, never go anywhere and order chicken. Always order the most expensive thing they have on the menu because you can eat chicken any damn where."

So, while I was getting closer to my dad, enjoying being spoiled to death and feeling somewhat like I had an ally in my corner, things at my mom's house were not so good.

My attitude was the worst. I wasn't trying to hear anything from my mom, we bumped heads about everything. I used to look at my mom and think, *I don't want to be anything like her, I'd never have this many kids if I couldn't take care of them, I'd never put a man before my kids, and I'd never settle for less.*

Our relationship was so bad she kicked me out for the first time when I was in 10th grade. I still remember her calling my dad (who was in LA at the time) telling him he better send somebody to come get 'this bitch'. She kicked me out again when I was in 11th grade.

Although I was happy with all the material possessions I was being spoiled with, emotionally, I was like a brick wall. Very cold, and heartless.

I never cried or showed emotion about anything. To me, that seemed weak. I also was very private talking about my issues. What I was feeling was off limits. I wasn't an emotional wreck crying over boys either like most teenage girls. Actually, I didn't feel emotionally attached to anyone, not even my dad.

Little did I know, I was about to reconnect with the young man who would change my life forever.

We initially met when I was in 8th grade. He was a varsity basketball player at the high school, which was next door to the middle school I attended. He and the other players would come to the middle school games and all the girls would look, point, and get googly eyed over them.

He sat behind me at a game once and I wasn't paying him any mind at all. To get my attention he started throwing little pieces of a pencil at my back until I turned around. Then he asked if he could come down to talk to me. That was how it began. He quickly became my boyfriend, but you know how middle school relationships go. We dated about a month and that was that.

I'd started high school off in College Park at North Clayton. My mom allowed me to go to the high school in our old neighborhood with my older sister who was a senior. Going to North Clayton with my sister was so much fun. I connected with a lot of childhood friends from Riverdale that I hadn't seen since elementary school and my first year of middle school, and because my sister was a senior, I got to hang with her and her friends most of the time. North Clayton was an all-black school on the southside of Atlanta and it was an epicenter of black urban culture, which was totally different from the middle school in Morrow I transferred from.

At North Clayton three things were taken very seriously: The Band, The Drama/Theater Department, and the epic rivalry games against Riverdale High School. The North Clayton vs. Riverdale games were a huge deal! I mean, you needed a new outfit and everything to go to the game.

During football season, the games would be at Twelve Oaks stadium and my favorite part would be the halftime show. I loved watching the marching band. I can still hear Outkast's *Spottieottiedopaliscious* being played by the band on the field with the divas upfront dancing with their flags, and the drum majors in the center killing it. During basketball season, the North Clayton vs. Riverdale games would sell out. The whole gym would be packed. People would be sitting on the floor, and there would be crowds of people outside hoping to get a peek in.

Celebrities would come to the games and everything. I remember Monica and C-Murda coming to one of the games. The basketball games were my favorite because they would be so crunk. Every time somebody dunked, in unison the whole gym would say, "U Aaaaaaa"! The cheerleaders would be in the stands stomping hard doing cheers against each other. I loved that energy so much I decided to try out for the cheerleading team. My oldest sister had been captain before graduating the year prior, so I was excited to follow in her footsteps.

I tried out and made the varsity team but only cheered for a very brief time because after my sister graduated, it was too difficult for me to get back and forth to school. So, my mom made me transfer back to the high school in our area and that's where *he* and I re-connected.

When I transferred from North Clayton, I was very upset. I hated everything about Morrow. In comparison to North Clayton, it was so lame. Morrow High was considered a "white" school even though it was in the same county as North Clayton. I remember thinking to myself, *I don't want to talk to anyone that goes to this lame ass school.* I eventually connected with some of my old middle school friends and through the grapevine heard my old boyfriend was checking for me.

He was from the East coast, his mother from Paterson, New Jersey, and his dad from Queens. So, he rocked Timbs, Wallabee's, Avirex jackets, and army fatigues. He was quiet and his swag was different from all the other guys. In the beginning it was like we were best friends. I'd go to his games, we'd go to the movies on the weekend, or I'd hangout at his house. His childhood was like mine. His mom's family was Muslim. His uncle, who he was very close with, was doing a 20-year bid, and he'd grown up without his mother and had a not-so-nice stepparent too. So, I could talk to him about stuff I would never talk about with other people. I guess you can say our similar traumatic experiences attracted me to him and we both had a love for hip-hop music. Cam'ron's *SDE* was our shit.

We became inseparable. He was at my house all the time, or I was at his. His dad would pick me up to ride with him to his away games, and he would even hang out with me and my dad. One time we were eating at an Italian restaurant in Buckhead. I'd ordered Lamb chops and I remember him trying to find the cheapest dish he could because he didn't want to be presumptuous. He ordered pasta and my dad reminded him he could order whatever he wanted. So, he changed his order and got a steak.

He was the first person I got high with. We were on the side of my mom's house, smoking. We got high as hell, ate

43

a whole box of Cinnamon Toast Crunch, and died laughing at everything.

At first, we were not these horny toads trying to do it all the time. We just enjoyed being around each other. That changed when he started spending the night at my house. My older sister had dated her high school boyfriend for a while and my mom used to let him spend the night, so my boyfriend started doing the same thing. That was one of the things I did like about my mom… she gave us a very long leash and she was very liberal about most things.

It wasn't long before I got pregnant. The first time I got pregnant I knew right away I had to get an abortion, then it happened again within a matter of months. After the second experience, I got on birth control, but being a reckless teen, I let my birth control refill lapse without letting my mom know. A year later I found myself in the same situation, but this time I decided to go through with the pregnancy. I was only 16 years old and he was 17. We were two kids about to have a kid of our own.

Prior to me getting pregnant, my mom had kicked me out because of my attitude. I went to stay with my dad in Buckhead. He had a penthouse condo with a panoramic view of the whole city. It was nice but my dad was ripping and running (as he called it) most of the time. So, I was there by myself. I was so far from my boyfriend and bored out of my mind. So, after a few months of staying in Buckhead I ended up apologizing to my mom so she would let me come back.

I got my driver's license shortly after moving back in with my mom and my dad bought me a brand-new Ford Mustang. It was black with white racing stripes on the side, and boyyyy, you couldn't tell me shit. I'd been seeing some of my other classmates roll up to school in their cars and I'd been patiently waiting to pull up in mine. I still remember the day I pulled into my high school parking lot in that

Mustang. People were coming outside like I was a star or something. It was crazy.

But all good things come to an end, right? I had my Mustang for 7 months before getting pregnant. As soon as my dad found out, he took my car back for good. He barely talked to me the entire time I was pregnant. He was really upset and embarrassed by it. My mom was supportive, but she let it be known that this was my child and she would not be responsible for raising it.

I wasn't the girl people expected to become a teen mom and some people verbalized their disappointment in me. I had teachers pulling me aside telling me it would ruin my life and that I'd never graduate or go to college. People look at you differently when you're a pregnant teen. They count you out and predict you'll have 5 kids before 25, be on food stamps, and live on Section 8 for the rest of your life. But from a very young age I always believed in myself and I knew having a child wasn't going to stop me from doing anything.

My pregnancy wasn't hard. It somewhat helped me develop a better relationship with my mom, and my older sisters were there for me the entire time too. My boyfriend came to all my doctors' appointments, and his family was very supportive as well. I was relatively small until the end of the term. It's like my stomach blew up overnight. I had a huge baby shower. You know, old-school style in my mom's den. My older sister decorated the entire downstairs, I had a huge cake, my mom made her famous baked spaghetti and garlic bread, and my aunt made the cutest cloth diaper party favors. We played all the traditional baby shower games and I got so many gifts it was insane. I got a highchair, car seat/stroller combo, rocking chair, swing, diaper Jeanie, and tons of blue and green newborn clothes for my little guy on the way.

Shortly after my baby shower I decided to stop going to school until after my son was born. I was too big and sitting at a desk all day was too uncomfortable. So, my boyfriend would bring my work after school and I'd send it back with him so he could turn it in for me.

My due date had come and gone, and my son was still inside baking. I was so tired of being pregnant. My nose was wider than all outdoors, I would get the worst Charlie horse pains in my legs when I stretched in the morning, my stomach looked like it would pop if you poked it and sleeping comfortably was over. I called my OB-GYN to ask about inducing my labor and was told if he didn't come within the next 14 days of me calling, they would induce.

I started walking every day to try to induce my own labor. After about 10 days my aunt told me about something she saw on TV where a woman said eating eggplant would induce labor. So, we made eggplant parmesan that night, and to my surprise, I went into labor. Til this day I'm not sure if it was really the eggplant or not though.

Me, my mom, and my son's father arrived at Southern Regional hospital together, and my dad arrived a few hours later. They all stayed the entire time. My labor was grueling. Although my water hadn't broken and I wasn't dilated much, they decided to admit me because I was already overdue. They made me walk every 30 minutes around the freezing cold hospital in my robe to speed up dilating. I remember being so tired and hungry and I was only allowed to eat ice and broth. I was in labor about 20 hours before I got an epidural, and at the 34th hour it was time for me to push. My OB-GYN was out of town on my delivery date, so I had a midwife deliver my son, and this woman was amazing. She was so patient; she was determined for me to have a vaginal birth without having a C-section or an episiotomy. I pushed for 2 hours straight and on Thursday, November 21, 2002 at

7:34am, I gave birth to a 10lbs, 2oz baby boy. (or sumo wrestler rather)

But when he came out, I didn't hear anything. The whole room was silent. I was still lying back so I couldn't see anything either. I remember asking my mom why he wasn't crying, and she looked at me as if she'd seen a ghost.

No one said anything for what seemed like forever. Then, I heard them saying his umbilical cord had been wrapped around his neck. They told me they had to take him off to another room. My dad was outside of the room while I pushed but he followed them into the room where they took my son.

According to my mom, my son was limp and blue when he was born. She said she thought he was dead. My dad said when they took him off to the other room, they stuck an instrument down his throat and stabilized his breathing.

They brought him to me about 30 minutes later all cleaned up. He looked like a fat Buddha man. His eyes were chinky just like mine were when I was born, and his head was full of slick jet-black hair. He had so much hair you couldn't even see his scalp

He had his fist in his mouth. The nurse said, "You can feed him NOW! He is hungry."

My mother had nursed all of us and all the other women in my family nursed as well. So naturally, I knew nursing was the best option for my son. He latched on immediately, and to my surprise, I started getting random visitors at my room door. Word had gotten around the maternity ward that a 17-year-old girl just had a 10lbs baby and people wanted to see him and me. My mom said she ran into one of the janitors down the hall and he asked if she was kin to the girl that had the 10lbs baby. My mom laughed and told him Yes! That's my grandson. That day my life changed forever. I was no longer a 17-year-old kid. I was a mother responsible for another human being's life.

My son brought so much joy to our family. Everyone loved him so much. He was so fat and juicy he looked like the Michelin tire man; he had so many rolls. He was such a good baby! He never cried unless he was hungry, and he was sleeping through the night before he was a month old. He was like a fat little man born into this world already wise. My dad would always say, "I'm telling you, this boy has been here before."

His great grandmother Gigi would call and ask for me to bring him over and everyone wanted their turn babysitting.

After my son's birth I had one more semester of high school. I would only go to school on Tuesdays and Thursdays most weeks, and my son's dad would bring my work and turn it in for me.

On days I went to school, I would pump 3 full 8 oz. bottles for my son. He was greedy and would normally drink all 3 before I got home. When I got home from school I would nurse him immediately on one boob and pump a bottle to freeze on the other boob. I never used an electrical pump either. I hand pumped every single bottle my son ever drank. I nursed him for over a year. He never once in his life drank baby formula. I did this all while still in high school, though my breasts would get so engorged on days I went. I hated that, which is why I went as little as possible.

I would always start leaking at school. I'd have to go in the bathroom and pump into the toilet when my breasts were uncomfortably engorged. A lot of people thought I wasn't going to graduate because I never came to school. My homeroom teacher even pulled me aside one day to express her concern. I assured her I had it under control and would be graduating for sure.

I was completely over the high school stuff and most of the people I went to high school with. Shit was just different after I had my son. I only went to prom because my mom begged me to go. She said I'd regret it if I didn't go. I went and *so* could've skipped it. Me and my date were already parents so there was no thrill. I was worried about getting the hell up out of there before my boobs started leaking. I didn't care about dinner before, or partying after. I just wanted to get back to the house to my son. We left prom, went to Waffle House, and went the hell home.

In June of 2003, I nursed my son at the kitchen table and pumped a bottle before heading to my high school graduation. I walked across the stage that night with my parents, all my siblings, my aunts, uncles, cousins, and my son in the stands.

I told myself I would graduate on time and I did!

Part 2: Caterpillar (Young Adult)

6

∞

Movin' On

After graduation I knew I did not want to go right to college like my other classmates. I needed to work, save some money, and get me a car for starters. And from there, go to school. Again, people questioned my decision. Even my mom felt if I didn't go straight to college I would never go. I remember her breaking down the statistics of what happens when kids don't start college right after high school. I told her once, and once only, I am going to go and when I go, I am going to finish it straight through.

I started working at a home goods store and I knew very early on that working a regular job was not going to cut it for me. I was too much of a rebel. I hated rules, and I hated being told what to do. Plus, regular jobs didn't pay enough. But I needed a car.

After working at the home goods store about 6 months I got a car and decided to start looking for jobs where I could make more money.

I was working full-time at the home goods store and my son would stay at home with his dad. He and I remained in our relationship after high school, but I noticed some traits in him that didn't sit well with me.

For one, he wasn't really trying to do anything for himself. He was depending on me to do everything. He was also hanging with low life dudes that didn't have shit going on.

For two, he was a thief and pathological liar. I found out he stole clothes and shoes from both of my brothers, and there were several occasions where I had money come up missing. At first, I didn't want to believe he was a thief or that he would be trifling enough to steal from me or my family members, but he was, and I learned this wasn't new behavior.

Meanwhile, I was working full-time and studying for the SAT (which I never took in high school) so I could get into college within the next year.

He wanted to pursue rapping, which I supported because he was talented, but even that he wasn't doing seriously. It was more like a hobby. It got to where he'd ask to drop me at work so he could use my car. Some days I said no, other days I let him, but he wasn't using the car to try to go find a job or make something of himself. He just wanted to go hang and do nothing with his friends. He would make comments and show through his actions that he wasn't trying to do anything for himself, and I guess he thought I was the type of chick that was going to be okay with that.

By this time, I had men with careers, their own cars, and their own money approaching me. So, I knew I could do better, but more than that, I knew I couldn't stay with someone who didn't have ambition and goals.

His grandmother, whom we all called Nana, said to me once back then, "Y'all should get married and do the right thing now that the baby is getting bigger, so y'all are not shacking up."

She even said she'd pay for us to have a small wedding and everything. I appreciated the offer, but I knew even at the young age of 18 that I did not want to marry him —even if we did have a child together. Don't get me wrong, during those first two years he didn't have a job, a car, or any money, but he was there for our son. He was a good father. He changed diapers, gave baths, cooked, and went to doctor appointments. So, I stayed with him for the sake of our son.

Once I got my car, I knew I wanted a better paying job, so I got on my grind looking. I had a cousin working at Hooters downtown on Peachtree street and she said she was making about $100 or more in tips a day. So, I went down, applied, and I got hired on the spot.

I worked at Hooters Tuesday-Saturday night. Normally, I'd let my son's dad drop me and he'd pick me up after. I was making good money at Hooters. On average, I was making $100 per night and when we had big conventions in town, I had some $300 plus nights.

Working downtown was exciting! When it was slow, all the Hooters girls would stand out on Peachtree street. We would see dudes in Box Chevys on 24's bumping T.I.'s "ASAP" and dudes driving Range Rovers bumping Usher's "Yeah, Damn" breaking their necks to get a look at us. Then you'd have the college girls bumping Ciara's "Goodies". I still remember the first time I heard "Goodies". I was so proud of Ciara and I wasn't surprised at all she had an energy about her even when we were young like she knew she was going to be a star. I'd met Ciara when I was in middle school. We were roomies at cheer camp in high school, I used to go to her house after practice sometimes, we'd talk on the phone after school, and my dad gave her a ride home from practice a few times when we cheered together . I hadn't talked to her since high school, but it was dope seeing someone I knew blow up like that.

Working at Hooters was fun. We had the reputation of being the "black" Hooters. My favorite part of work was hearing stories from the other girls who were dating athletes and entertainers.

Although the money was good, I never really had the temperament for being a waitress. I was bad at being fake and bubbly, which is what being a Hooters girl is all about.

Working at Hooters you have men trying to holla at you all day, and I would be so mean to them. Ironically that made them tip me even more. I was known as the mean Hooters Girls and I had dudes that would come in every weekend and request to sit with my mean ass.

One time, me and my cousin were at a Falcons game and as we were leaving this guy said, "Oh shit, that's that mean ass Hooters girl right there!"

We both died laughing. You better believe he was in there at one of my tables the following weekend.

After working there a few months I saved up some money and me and my son's dad moved into an apartment together. When we moved together our relationship got worse. I could see more and more that he had no plans of changing and he became very insecure and jealous. Plus, he could not keep a job.

I worked at Hooters during the height of BMF. For those who don't know, BMF was the largest black drug cartel in the history of the United States. Led by Demetrius "Big Meech" Flenory, they had the whole city on lock. There were a few Hooters girls fucking with dudes in BMF, but the whole time I worked there I was never checking for any of the high-profile dudes that came in there.

I'd just applied to Clayton State University and gotten accepted, and I was due to start spring semester. So, my plan was to stack up so I could work less days and go to school full-time.

We got a new manager at Hooters and he was a chauvinist, racist asshole; all the girls hated him. We were the "Black" Hooters and we all know most Hooters restaurants are not predominantly black. He didn't like that at all. Even the white girls we did have working there were just about all dating black men and he *really* hated that.

One day, after our shift meeting, he changed my tables for no reason. He took the four tables I had up front and gave them to another girl he was rumored to be dating. He reassigned me to some crappy tables in the back. He overheard me talking to my cousin about how upset I was because it was a Saturday night and no one wanted the back tables on a Saturday night. He literally put his head in the middle of our conversation out of nowhere and yelled, "If you don't like it, clock out and leave!"

Back then, I was a hothead with a quick explosive temper, I'd cuss anybody out and when I went off, I went off. I was already pissed and in that moment with him just jumping in my face out of nowhere, my mind went blank and I cussed him the fuck out right there in front of everyone. I called him every fat, white, cracker in the book. Needless to say, that was my last day at Hooters.

On my drive home it hit me. Like, fuck, I won't make that kind of money at no other restaurant. What am I going to do now?

I hated waitressing but loved the money. So, I sucked up my pride and went and applied at an Olive Garden close to where I lived. I got the job but within 3 weeks I quit. The food wasn't expensive enough and it wasn't a fun environment like Hooters, so the tips were horrible. I wasn't going to be able to survive and pay my bills at a regular restaurant, so the hunt for a better job was back on.

Things with my son's dad continued to get worse. I was sick of him using my car, laying around, and not having money to do for our son. We'd gotten to where we argued all the time and our altercations had begun getting physical where we'd fight each other, so I knew it was time to end it.

For me, it was a cold turkey break. There were no tears and no back and forth. It was just over. I had completely outgrown him mentally, and honestly, I was relieved to be free of him. I didn't feel any sadness. I wasn't concerned with who he'd date next. I just wanted to focus on my son, school, and making money.

He took it hard. He would blow up my phone crying, leave a million messages begging me back, show up to my house unannounced. But going back wasn't an option. I did want him to continue being a good father though. I knew he didn't have a job, so I wasn't even pressing him for money. I knew I was about to start school and I needed him to be there for our son, but after trying to get me back for months with no luck, he fell back from me and our son. He stopped calling to check on him and he stopped being reliable. I couldn't depend on him or trust his word when it came to our son.

A good while had passed after quitting the restaurant and I still hadn't found another job. I was getting a little stressed out because I had bills to pay.

Things were about to look up though, in a way I never expected.

7

∞

Dancin' for Money

My sister, who'd been a stripper for about 3 years, ended up inviting me to her birthday party at the club where she danced. I'd never been to the strip club; I always felt it wasn't really my thing, but I agreed to go. She worked at this small club downtown that I'd never even heard of. I knew about Magic City, Strokers, and Blue Flame from working at Hooters where the running joke was being a Hooters girl is just one step away from being a stripper. And I'd heard all the strip club stories from the Hooter girls that were with dudes in BMF. I heard about BMF shutting down Magic. There were stories about strippers leaving work with black hefty bags full of money. Atlanta was lit back then! Outside of the strip clubs, clubs like Visions, 112, and Essos were popping, or so I heard. I was only 18, I was already a mom, and the club scene just wasn't my thing.

I knew my sister and her friends were making money dancing but that was something I just couldn't fathom doing. I was way too shy, for one and self-conscious about my body. After having my son, I had a few tiger stripes on my stomach that I hated. So, dancing was out of the question for me...or so I thought.

Her birthday was on a Saturday night. I still remember walking in that club like it was yesterday. The club was a small hole in the wall, but it was jam packed. It was dimly lit and cloudy from weed and cigarette smoke. Money was everywhere! There were two naked women on stage, one sliding down the pole and the other on the stage floor face down, ass up. The music was so loud I could barely hear my own voice, but it was all such a thrilling sight!

I came with my cousins, mom and close friends. We had a table reserved for us and soon after we sat down, we had drinks coming our way from across the room. There were two older gentlemen in their late 40's sitting across the room and they asked me and my cousin to come over.

One of the guys was black, the other guy was white. The white guy signaled for me to come over. When I got over to him, he said he saw me as soon as I walked in and couldn't believe how beautiful I was. He asked the waitress to come over and he ordered a couple hundred dollars in *ones*. When she returned with the *ones*, he put $200 in my hand to go throw on stage. He kept putting *ones* in my hand all night. If I walked off from him, he'd find me and put more ones in my hand. I ended up leaving the club with a couple hundred dollars in my purse. I was like wow!!!

The next day I said to myself, *Damn, that would be the perfect place for me to work.* I was against stripping, but I was totally for waitressing. I thought about it for a few days then went up to the club to talk to the manager. He hired me on the spot as a waitress, but he also informed me that the permit to waitress is the same price as the permit to dance. (Yes, you need a permit to dance, and in the city of Atlanta, you need a separate permit for each club where you work.) Stripping is a legit business. Permits back then were $350 and I hadn't been consistently working since quitting my last job, so my money was tight.

He said, "And you're about to start school too, right? Your schedule will be more flexible if you dance."

I had a mental debate in my head right there. I knew what he was saying was true, but I could not see myself dancing. So, back and forth I went in my head, but I still decided to stick with just waitressing.

He said, "Look, I'm just going to be honest with you. It's not always as busy as it was when you came for the party. It's going to be harder to make your money in here as a waitress."

Then he put some icing on the cake. He said, "If you dance, I'll buy the permit for you."

I thought about it for a few minutes and said, "Fuck it, I'll dance! I went and applied for the permit that day.

I immediately went and talked to my sister after I applied for the permit. It was a Tuesday afternoon and Friday was going to be my first night. So, she gave me a crash course on the strip club. Here were the rules:

-Don't trust any of the girls; they're not your friends.
-Don't be in there getting drunk.
-Don't ever leave with no dude — no matter what!

That was the gist of our conversation. After I asked her where I should go to get my dance outfits and shoes, she told me about *Looks of Atlanta* and a few other shops. I went and bought a few outfits, a garter belt, and a pair of black patent leather 6-inch stripper heels. While trying on outfits I started becoming very self-conscious about my body. Yeah, my stomach was flat and I had a slim and shapely figure, but I still had a lot of body shame. Prior to having my son, I didn't have a stretch mark on my body and now I was super aware of them. I kept thinking no one was going to want me to dance looking like this. I decided I would wear tight bodycon dresses instead of two pieces because I felt more comfortable with how they looked on my body. After an hour of trying on outfits I was all set for my first night.

Before my first night I decided to come up with my own set of rules to go by as a dancer and I picked my name. My rules were:

1. **Don't get involved with a strip club dude.**
2. **Never tell any of the girls my personal business.**
3. **Never get possessive over the customers.**
4. **Never drink or smoke.**

I knew I needed to have a plan and I knew I needed to be completely sober if I was going to do this. I was going into an environment full of money, drugs, liquor, men, and naked women from walks of life I knew nothing about. I knew anything could go wrong at any time and I needed to be sharp, focused, with my ears and eyes open always.

And I decided to go by the name... Cherokee.

On my first night, I remember pulling into the parking lot. My bag was in the truck, and my stomach was full of butterflies. I had on a grey skirt, a black tank top, and some black slide-in sandals. I walked in with my bag rolling behind me. It was around 9 p.m. There were already people in the club, but it wasn't packed yet.

I walked through the door and my heart was beating a million times per second. As I was making my way to the back, a guy got up from his table and told me to come see him first after I got dressed. On the way back I checked in with the DJ to make sure he knew about the agreement I made with the manager when I got hired. I told the manager I was not comfortable going on stage and I'd let him know when I was ready.

When I walked into the dressing room it was full of naked women laughing, talking, and catching up on the latest gossip as they put on their makeup and outfits. I didn't say anything to anybody. I just found an empty locker and started getting undressed. My sister came in shortly after and I was so relieved to see her. She was dating one of the club managers so she could come and go as she pleased, and she didn't have to pay a bar fee like the rest of the girls. Bar fee is what you pay each night in order to work at the club. The bar fee was normally between $45-55, and you had to tip out the DJ and the House mom each night too. The House mom was there to provide hygiene products and keep the girls in line. So, each night, with bar fee and tip out combined, you were expected to pay around $75.

My sister had been there a while. She was one of the top money makers and she could dance her ass off. So, the other girls respected her and after they saw us talking, they wanted to know who I was. She let everyone know I was her sister.

The first outfit I put on was a black bodycon dress with rhinestones on it. After getting dressed, spraying myself with perfume, and putting a fresh piece of gum in my mouth, I walked out on the floor.

The guy who told me to come see him immediately waived me over. This was it... I was about to give my first dance.

I was so nervous walking over to him. I mean, I had rhythm but never considered myself to be a great dancer like my sister. Plus, stripping was a different type of dancing. Knowing how to make your butt clap and knowing how to do the stripper two-step is a work of art, and you don't just learn how to do it overnight. Stripping is not just about taking your clothes off; it's a cerebral seduction. I'd practiced a little bit at home in the mirror, but still felt shy and self-conscious as I made my way over to him.

61

In Atlanta, dancers get fully naked, but on my first dance I didn't even take my dress all the way off. I just pulled the bottom up and the top down and started dancing for him.

Dances were $10 a song and the first song I danced to was Jeezy and Mannie Fresh's, "And Then What". As the song was coming to an end the guy signaled with his hand in a circular motion for me to dance another song. The second song I danced to was, D4L's, "Laffy Taffy". I remember thinking like, damn this is a lot to pay attention to. I have to dance, be sexy, and count songs to keep up with my money?

As the second song came to an end, he signaled for me to dance again. The next song was Mr. Big Tyme's, "Check My Footwork". He continued signaling with his hand until I danced 10 songs. In the strip club they don't play the whole song, so I made my first $100 within 30 minutes. After I finished dancing for him, I had guys signaling for me to come to them next from every direction.

I danced what seemed nonstop for the rest of the night, only pausing briefly so I could freshen up in the back. I worked from 10pm -3am. I made $800 that first night and I couldn't believe that shit. Getting home pouring all that cash on the floor and counting it was like a rush I'd never felt before. I was like, damn, I should've been doing this!!!

After that first night, I came up with a plan. I would give myself four years— tops to dance. I'd only do it until I graduated from college. I came up with a nightly quota for myself, which was making at least $500. I would only work at the small low-key club where I was because I didn't want anybody to know I was a stripper. It was my secret. To the outside world I was a mother and full-time student, but for those who *knew me* knew me, I was a mother, full-time student, and on Thursday-Saturday night, I was in the strip club getting to the money.

Back then, the culture of stripping was different. It was like a secret society; you didn't tell people you danced. There were no camera phones, no social media, and stripping damn sure wasn't glorified. In fact, you couldn't bring phones in the club— period —unless you paid security, and as camera phones came on the scene, if you were caught recording, in-club security would take your phone and throw you out. You might even get yo ass beat.

The club I worked at was a small hole in the wall but me, my sister, and my cousin that I'd previously worked with at Hooters was now with us at the club too; and we were making a lot of money in that muthafucka! I knew I could've been making more at a bigger club like *Magic City* or *Body Tap* but I didn't want to be on the scene like that or known as a stripper.

Prior to becoming a stripper I'd never been to a strip club so where I was at was all I knew. Eventually I went to some of the other clubs and, yes indeed, they were making way more money, but I also noticed something else that was weird. It was like all the girls had these big plastic looking asses that didn't quite fit their bodies right at the other clubs. I'd never even heard of buttshots, but I remember leaving one of the other strip clubs one night thinking how the fuck do all these chicks got these asses that look the same. Nobody at the small club I worked at had buttshots, so it was something I'd never seen.

After I'd been dancing for a couple of months, I had money stacked, my bills were paid, I was doing good in school, and I'd gotten through my first semester with 3 A's and a B. I was already into my second semester when I met the second man that would change my life.

63

8

∞
_____   _____

Along Came the Marine

My mindset was different than most of the young college kids on campus. I was already a mother and I was already making more money than my college professors. I wasn't there to go to keg parties, or pledge to sororities; I wanted no part of "college" life.

I was fresh out of a five-year relationship, so dating was the last thing on my mind. I was there to do my work and that was it. I sat in the front row of all my classes, I didn't talk to anyone at all on campus. I just did my work and left.

That was until I was walking through the parking lot toward the main campus one day and this guy in a brand-new white Monte Carlo SS with the sunroof open pulled up on me with his shades on. I guess he thought he was Superfly or some shit.

He said, "Hi."

I quickly returned his greeting and kept walking, rolling my eyes. In my head, I was like, *Damn he's lame.*

I got to class and as I was pulling my notebook out, I saw the guy from the parking lot walk in. He still had his shades on and I'm thinking, *Oh great! This lame is in my class.*

After class, he approached me, asked my name, and asked if he could walk with me to my next class. I told him no, I was about to leave. He asked where I was headed, and I told him the bank.

So, the next class, he did the same thing and I turned him down again. The third time he said, "Well, if I can't walk you to class, can I walk with you to your car?"

I agreed, because at this point, I'm annoyed.

I said, "But I'm in a rush. I have somewhere to be before 1'o clock."

He said, "Lemme guess... the bank?"

I laughed and said, "Yes."

"Damn, you go to the bank a lot!" He said. "What do you do; you must dance or something?"

I was kind of stunned when he said it. I guess my face gave it away. He started laughing again.

"It's nothing wrong with that," he said. "If that's how you make your money, that's cool."

He asked for my number and I said no but he would not give up. This dude was persistent!

After doing this dance for a few weeks I gave in and gave him my number, not because I was interested, but because I was sick of him asking. I never answered when he called. Then I'd have to try and avoid him at school.

I mean, he was tall, brown-skinned, handsome, tatted up, with pretty, light auburn-brown eyes. He drove a nice car too. I could tell he was used to having girls swoon all over him, but I just wasn't interested. So, I had no intention of answering any of his calls.

One night I was having girl talk with my sisters and he called and left a voicemail. I felt kind of bad, like, damn this dude has called me a million times and I haven't answered. Let me just call him back this once.

After I dialed, I was secretly hoping he would not answer. I just wanted him to see I made the effort. But he answered on the first ring and we ended up talking for three hours straight, just like middle school kids or something. We talked about everything. You know, the typical shit you talk about when you're getting to know someone new. He told me he'd seen me on the first day of class and that the first time he saw me, he said to himself that I was going to be his wife. He said he would be home in his spare time thinking of what he could say to get my attention because I never turned around in class.

After our 3-hour conversation he asked if I could meet him before class the next day so we could talk in person and I agreed. We met the next day and chopped it up more in person before class. After class, he had to go to work but asked if he could see me when he got off. I agreed.

He lived close to campus and I lived 10 minutes away from him so when he got off work that night I went over to his place and we chilled, talked, watched movies, smoked, and kissed all night like some teenagers and he was one of those dudes who swore kissing wasn't really his thing that he didn't even like kissing like that but he kissed me first. After that night we were literally together every day.

Being with him was much different than being with my son's dad. He was older, he'd been in the military, so he'd traveled, had a job, and a car. He could actually afford to take me out, which he did every weekend. We were very physically attracted to each other too. We were like magnets for one another. I wasn't used to being publicly affectionate, but he brought that side out of me. He was very affectionate, and I could tell he was proud of having me as his girl.

He was very funny and charming. He would have me dying laughing all day and we never argued about anything. He wanted me with him all the time. He'd ask me to come to the barbershop, the carwash, family dinners, to hang out with him and his friends. Our sexual chemistry was like something out of a porn movie. We had sex every single day multiple times a day and we never got tired of each other. It was like each time the sex got better! When we had epic nights, we would look at each other afterwards and say, "History Books". That was our inside joke.

It felt like we were best friends and lovers at the same time. He would say, "You're my girlfriend, but you're, like, my homeboy too. Most girls would've gotten on my nerves by now if I had them around me like this, but it's something about you."

I used to catch him staring at me and he would say, "Man, who are you and where did you come from?"

Our relationship felt magical, our chemistry just felt natural and organic. He took me out a lot and when we were out, complete strangers would come up and tell us how good we looked together.

He used to always say, "You know I loved you when I first saw you, right?"

And I would roll my eyes and laugh. We complimented each other well and I was happy with him.

Me dancing wasn't really an issue at first honestly. The first few months of us dating I'd slacked off a lot from work. I was only working about 1 day per week because I was spending so much time with him.

I still remember the first time he said 'I love you' to me. I didn't say it back and I tried to break up with him after. The whole love thing was awkward for me; it always had been something in me that resisted too much love, affection, and emotion when it came to men. So, I completely shut down after he said it and ignored his calls for a few days, but he was adamant about not allowing me to break up with him

Once feelings were involved, he started making comments here and there about me dancing. Asking when I planned on stopping and just letting it be known that he didn't like the idea of his girl stripping. I let him know, straight up, that I was a single parent and full-time student. I was already doing this before him, so he knew what the deal was. There's no other legal job I could've done and made this type of money. Stopping was not an option. I mean, he was doing better than the average 20-something year old, but he was in no position to pay my bills. And I knew how to handle myself in the strip club. I wasn't your "typical" stripper, I handled that shit with a professional business mind, I was all about the money, not hooking up with niggas, getting drunk or having small talk.

So, I felt he had no right to ask me to stop.

I was enjoying the money I was making but the strip club can be a very ruthless environment. To me, it was the female version of being a drug dealer, except it was legal. Still, the mindset was the same. Strippers become very territorial over the customers to the point of fighting each other in the dressing room. You had girls snorting cocaine in the bathroom, girls turning tricks in VIP, girls with real live pimps. Like *real* pimps with fur coats and candy curls and shit, who come in to make sure they are making money.

So it's a lot going on and when are you new to a club, and the other dancers can feel your presence (meaning they feel a shift in their money because now the dudes that used to dance them or break bread with them are now dancing you and breaking bread on you) shit can get ugly... real ugly. There's a lot of envy, hate, and greed in the club and if you're not mentally strong that environment can chew you up and spit you out.

***

It was a Saturday night. I was at work and it was dead, which was kind of odd because the night before it'd been super busy, one of those epic nights me, my sister, and my cousin had racked up something serious. Normally, when my sister racked up you wouldn't see her for a few weeks. She was almost finished with school and she'd danced long enough to save a lot of money, so she only came to work here and there. My cousin was going to a concert that night, so I was at work solo. I'd been slacking off due to my relationship, so I was trying to run it up two nights in a row. So, there I was sitting to myself debating on if I felt like paying the fine to leave early, which was $75. I was about to say, fuck it, and pay it. I wasn't about to sit there freezing all night making no money. To my surprise, my sister walked in. She was on the same vibe as me, like, shit last night was so epic, I'm trying to rack up again. Once she got on the floor and saw how slow it was, she was like let's get the fuck out of here.

I'd been dancing for almost a year and I'd never had any drama with anybody. I was sticking to my rules and everything was cool.

Now I'd dealt with my fair share of hate from other females since I was a kid. Jealousy from other girls was present from the time I was in kindergarten, but it didn't get blatant and nasty until around 6th grade. That was when I really noticed and realized girls pre-judged and were jealous of me just because. During my first year of middle school I remember going to the bathroom, closing the stall door, and seeing *KEBA IS A STUCK-UP BITCH* written in black permanent marker. I was like damn that's how you feel??? I had no clue who wrote it and I knew for sure I hadn't done anything to anybody.

Something I never understood was how someone could conclude that you were stuck up without even knowing you?

That was what most females thought of me. Well the ones who didn't personally know me.

It continued through high school and my adult life too. I would see, *Keba is a bitch* on desks, in books, and bathroom stalls. When I would hear through the grapevine what a chick said about me it was always the same thing: *she's stuck-up... she thinks she's all that... she's a bitch.*

I was always an introverted and very shy person. I always sat back and observed, and I was never trying to fit in. I wasn't afraid of anybody, and I spoke my mind, so some people took that as me being stuck up. However, anyone who knew me knew I was one of the coolest, most down-to-earth people.

Senior year, right before graduation, this chick told me, "I'm so glad I got to know you, you are nothing like I thought you were going to be."

I said, "What did you think I would be?"

She made a face as if it pained her to say what she was about to say. Then she replied, "Honestly, I thought you were going to be a stuck-up bitch."

I'd experienced being treated rudely for no reason by bank tellers and cashiers. I'd had rumors spread about me and gotten the evil eye from women more times than I could count. I had a chip on my shoulder about it too and I could be a mean ass bitch. It got to the point where I was ready to go off on or fight any female who felt she could disrespect me because she was bothered by my existence. But I'd never experienced anything on the level of what I was about to experience this night at work…

Me and my sister went to the back to put our clothes on. We were both going to leave early. My sister's boyfriend was a manager and he let me skip on paying the fine that night, which I was super happy about. As we were in the back getting dressed, we noticed two other girls that neither of us ever associated with getting dressed too. We didn't think anything of it. We didn't talk to the girls who had pimps, or the girls who snorted coke in the bathroom, so we continued getting ready, like, whatever.

As we were walking out of the club, I was a few steps ahead of my sister. I was almost out of the door completely when she saw an old friend. She asked me to come back real quick while she talked to him so we could walk out together. Of course, I agreed, and we went back.

After she finished talking to her friend, we walked out together. As we walked out, one of the girls we saw getting dressed in the back approached me. She wasn't on no rowdy rah rah shit, but she asked me a question. I'm looking, like, *Huh, why are you even talking to me?* We've never said anything to each other before, so it was weird as fuck.

So, as she was talking to me, the other girl from the back swung on me out of nowhere. Fortunately, my sister caught her before she hit me. It was so crazy because right as my sister hit the girl who was trying to sneak me, my cousin walked up out of nowhere. She'd just so happened to stop by after the concert she was attending ended.

Just as I saw her, I swung and hit the girl in front of me. My cousin didn't blink twice, she immediately ran up and jumped in. The girl I was fighting grabbed my hair. Back then, my natural hair was really long, and I wore it bone straight. She didn't just grab it; she wrapped it around her hand twice, so she had a sumo grip on it. So, my head was completely down, and I was punching her wherever I could. It was 1:30 a.m. and five of us were brawling in the middle of the street.

Next thing I knew, I heard the voice of a man yelling, but I couldn't see him because she still had my hair and my head was down. The man yelling was their pimp and he ran up and pulled a gun on me, my sister and my cousin,

71

demanding for us to get off his hoes. By the time he pulled the gun, security had made their way out of the club to break us all up. They hopped in their car and drove off.

Later, I found out these girls had razor blades in their mouths and were planning to slice my face up all in the name of greed, envy, and hate. We were all blessed; none of us got seriously hurt. Other than a few broken nails and a handful of my hair missing, I was good and grateful to be alive. That shit could've gone so wrong for me. I went to work solo and both my sister and my cousin happened to show up at the right time. I knew some higher power had to have been protecting me.

That night, I really took heed to the environment I was in. Like, this shit was not a game at all. There were chicks in the club who came from the gutter, for real, with nothing to lose. A lot of the girls had pimps who beat their asses if they didn't make a certain amount of money. Some girls were turning tricks out of the club because they had to. Other girls were getting pimped and recruiting the new girls they could tell were weak minded. There were a lot of lost, hurt, and deeply broken women in the club willing to do whatever for the money.

I never went back to that hole in the wall club again after that, and my sister stopped dancing all together after the brawl. I took about a month off and just chilled. My boyfriend was really in my ear about stopping after the brawl because he was concerned about my safety. I felt where he was coming from, but I knew getting a regular job wasn't an option. So, I went to a different club that was much closer to where I lived. The new club was way more known than the club I'd been at before. It was bigger, there were way more girls, and it was dope boy central.

The perfect recipe to get to the bag.

9

∞

Runnin' Up A Check

The club I'd been at before was downtown and it was lowkey, so it was more of a professional crowd with a sprinkle of dope boys. This new club was all dope boys and a tiny sprinkle of professional guys. It stayed open later and the dances were $5 instead of $10, which I wasn't thrilled about, but that muthafucka would be rockin! I'm talking packed wall to wall, especially on Sunday nights and Tuesday nights.

I was making money before, but this club put me in a whole 'nother bracket. Because the dances were only $5, I would have dudes dance me 20-30 songs like it was nothing. Let the DJ put on Gucci Mane's, "Trap House" or Yola's, "Ain't Gon Let Up" and the whole club would go crazy. Money would be flying in the air from all directions, strippers literally jumping off stage to get the money that fell to the floor. The DJ would pause on this one part of, "Ain't Gon Let Up" and the whole club would yell in unison… "I JUST DON'T GIVE A FUCK!"

On nights like that you would see girls dancing in piles of money in every corner of the club. At the end of the night we were dumping the piles we made on stage but didn't have time to count on the floor in the dressing room in the back so we could divvy it up before going home. Let me explain further.

See, on a busy night, you and whoever else you went on stage with could make a couple thousand dollars easily. We weren't trying to count all that money after we got off stage. Shit, we were trying to get to the dressing room so we could freshen up and get back out on the floor and make more money!

Counting *ones* takes a lot of time. When I counted at the end of the night, my ones always had to be neat and facing the same direction, and I always kept a few big rubber bands in my purse too.

The drive through tellers at my bank used to hate to see me coming. They banned me from coming through the drive-up with so many *ones* because I would have to send the tube back and forth so many times. I was forced to go in (which I hated). I don't know why, but I didn't want people to see me with that much cash. The money smelled just like the strip club too, a combination of weed, cigarettes, and Black and Mild's. The tellers would always look at my stacks of *ones* with judgmental eyes. I know they wanted to ask so badly what I did for a living, but never had the guts.

This club was also buttshot central. Like 75% of the girls had buttshots. They were all going to some black-market lady doing the shots in hotel rooms. I was slim, but shapely. I didn't have a big butt or big boobs, but I still made a lot of money and I wasn't about to let no chick in a hotel room inject me with shit.

In that club it was a lot of pressure around having a fake butt and fake boobs, and a lot of girls caved under that pressure. Some went overboard and fucked their bodies up.

This club was closer to where I lived and where I went to school, so I saw a few people I knew from high school which I didn't like. I still wanted this to be something I

74

secretly did, but by this time I was like, whatever, I'm getting money!

However, once I saw my Political Science professor in the club one night, that fucked me up. I ran to the back and stayed back there until he left. I remember thinking and wondering, what the fuck was he doing there in that hood ass club. This wasn't a place for dorky professors.

I had some epic nights working there though. I remember these dudes from New York came in. They were drinking Henny and Red Bull all night. I was still sticking to my rules, so drinking was a no-go for me, but the more fucked up they got, the more money they threw. I danced for them the whole night. I was standing in a pile of *ones*. Next thing I knew, dude started throwing hundreds on the floor. He was drunk as shit. I wasn't complaining though. I made $2500 that night.

I was making 3x more than what I was making before, but I kept my expenses low. I was always in the mindset of dancing being temporary. I didn't want to build a lifestyle based around me being a stripper. What if I broke my leg or sprained my ankle and couldn't go to work? I wanted to ensure I could pay my bills even if I wasn't dancing, just in case, god forbid, I had to get a regular job. So as tempting as it was to hop in a Benz or move in a condo in the city, I stayed lowkey.

I was under the age of 21 making 6 figures in straight cash but my spending habits weren't outrageous. I shopped, spoiled my son to death, and ate out a lot. But mainly, I was stacking up for a rainy day. I'd given myself a time limit on dancing and wanted to pay off my car, pay off my credit cards, and move into a house before I stopped.

I'd moved to a new apartment. Me and my boyfriend were still together. He still had his own place but was at my house just about every night. He was the only guy I'd ever let be around my son and my son liked him a lot. After living there for a while, I gave him a key and all he did at his own house was basically go get more clothes so he could come back to my house.

My son was two years old, going on three, but he was one of those oddly wise kids. He just knew things most kids didn't. He picked up on things and knew how to articulate his words well. He knew how to read before he was three years old and you couldn't get nothing over on him. He never believed in Santa, the boogie man, the tooth fairy, or anything else you can use to bribe kids – and he questioned everything.

We used to read together every night before he went to bed, and he used to want to stay in the tub playing with his toys forever. Because I grew up in a household where my mom didn't really buy junk, nor did we ever have food in excess, and everything we bought was off-brand I did the complete opposite in my home.

I wanted my son to have all the snacks he wanted, and I never bought anything off-brand. Ever. My pantry would be loaded with all the snacks I wished we had when I was a kid. Pop Tarts, Fruit Roll Ups, Slim Jim's, chips, cookies, popcorn, Capri suns, and 3-4 different kinds of cereal. I would go overboard at the grocery store, and to be honest, I was happy I could go to the store and buy whatever the fuck I wanted with my own money, not food stamps.

When it came to spoiling my son, I went overboard too. His dad was very inconsistent by this time. My son would cry and ask why his dad hadn't called or seen him and I wouldn't know what to say. So, I would make up stuff like, "Oh, he probably lost his phone." Or, "He's out of town." Although I had zero respect for my son's dad, I never bashed him to my son. I knew my son would grow up and make his own decisions about his father. I didn't have to tell him anything negative. I would overcompensate for his dad not being there big time. All his clothes were name brand. I'd buy him 3-4 pairs of shoes at a time. He kept a fresh haircut, his birthdays were always huge, and he had all the *things* kids desired like Power Wheel trucks, PlayStation, and every other toy he wanted.

I took him to the circus, Chuck E Cheese, and the movies regularly. I just wanted him to have anything he wanted. During his early years, raising him was pretty easy. I was financially secure, and I had a lot of support from my family. Between my little sisters, my son's grandfather and great grandmother on his dad's side and my mom, I never had to put my son in daycare because they all took turns babysitting. I was so grateful for that.

Me and my son were very close. He had his own room but would come get in my bed every single night. On nights I worked I'd pick him up from my mom's then go home. We'd get in around 5 a.m. and I would leave him a pop-tart and a juice box on the table. He would get up, eat his snack, and turn on cartoons without even bothering me. He knew how to just chill and he never cried about anything.

My relationship, on the other hand, was no longer in the magical phase. Although we still loved to be around each other and our sexual chemistry was still on a trillion, with me being a dancer and him being the average young good looking 20-something year old, the drama had commenced. I found out about him cheating several times, I'd break up with him, he'd beg and plead for me to take him back, we'd fuck good and get back together, then I'd do some spiteful shit on the low like let a nigga take me out or give me some money without him knowing and that was our cycle.

I never fucked with anyone from the club like that, but I did give my number to a few of my regulars. That was just part of the game; I had to stay in communication with the dudes that came in and broke the most bread.

So, he always justified his cheating with me dancing, and I'd always go back to our original conversation: *You knew I was a dancer before you asked me to be your girl, stopping isn't an option.*

I knew he was still fucking with chicks behind my back so I would let dudes do things for me without him knowing. I had dudes giving me money, buying me perfume, shoes, bags, and taking me to dinner. In my mind it wasn't really cheating because I wasn't fucking any of them.

He never caught me doing anything, but he was always so concerned with me leaving him for a dude that had more money than him. So, we were in this tit for tat cycle and instead of just breaking up we continued to torture each other. He was like a moth to my flame. We basically drove each other crazy. He was a liar and a cheater, and I was spiteful and deceptive. He couldn't leave me alone if he wanted to and I couldn't resist him.

A few months would pass, and things would feel good in our relationship. Then, Boom! Here comes the drama with this nigga. I never shared my relationship drama with anyone. Everybody thought we were such a great couple but behind closed doors we were just taking turns hurting each other and using sex as the remedy to everything.

After a while I could see he was clearly not going to stop doing what he was doing so I pushed my boundaries a little farther. I had a dude on the side I would kick it with regularly. He and I were intimate with each other, but he knew what the deal was, and he was cool playing his role.

I knew I could get a man that had way more than him. I had doctors, lawyers, athletes, and entertainers pursuing me, but in my experience a lot of high-profile dudes were straight corny, super arrogant, and were used to chicks swooning. That was not me. Plus, I was never impressed with jewelry, cars, and bottles. I'd seen my dad with more so that shit was nothing to me.

I'd normally just let them take me shopping or to dinner at my favorite restaurants like the Oceanaire and Ruth Chris.

I got a kick out of not sleeping with them and still getting what I wanted. I learned very early on that you didn't have to sleep with dudes to get money or material possessions from them. Honestly, dudes never came at me like that. Even in the club they were always respectful. I would literally have dudes in the club tell me, "I can't even let you dance. You're the wife type. Imma just give you some bread." And they'd just put money in my hand without me having to do anything.

I would have men ask me to go on 5-star vacations and offer to buy me condos and cars. It was crazy!

Put it this way, I turned down way more than I accepted. I wasn't willing to let any ole body take me out or buy me things. I never accepted a vacation, and I never accepted any of the condos or cars I was offered.

I was never interested in just dating dudes because they had money. I had to have an honest attraction to a man and that was hard to come by, which is why it was so difficult to leave my relationship. We had this chemistry that was unmatched, even by dudes who had way more money and status than him.

In the strip club you would see rappers and athletes come through, but the dope boys were the real stars in the club. And the dope boys fucked with me heavy, especially the lowkey ones. Those were my favorites.

I loved the street niggas that never made it rain or got sections but would dance you the whole night and then pay

79

you 2 or 3x what they owed. Some of my best customers were dope boys and a lot of times we would end up talking about real shit while I was dancing for them.

I was always honest about having a boyfriend. They would love to say, "Man, how the hell yo nigga got you in here working??? If you were my girl ain't no way in hell you would be in here! You need to fuck wit a real nigga."

Although street niggas, dope boys, or whatever you wanted to call them have this tough macho façade, they really have a sweet side if you get to know them on a deeper level. They really wanna be in love but will never say it out loud, and it's too bad for them that the strip club is no place to come looking for love.

I had this one D Boy that would come in. He was a big dude and his pockets were even bigger. But he was quiet. He would slide in and out of the club real quick, but every time he came through, he broke major bread on me.

I rarely did VIP dances because I knew what most niggas were expecting when girls went to VIP. So, I always turned them down, but there was one big VIP section in the downstairs part of the club and the curtain was beaded so everyone could see through. He would always sit in that section. I didn't mind dancing for him there.

One night I was dead tired and decided to leave early. I was in the back getting dressed. I literally had one leg inside of my jeans when one of the girls came in and said, "Your guy just walked in and he's asking for you."

I took my jeans off so quick, put my dance outfit back on, and went right to his section. I started dancing. He dropped $1,000 in *ones* and dipped. That was how he moved.

10

∞
_____   _____

A Sugar Baby is Born

I always kept it business in the club. I was never possessive over the customers, I never tried to make anything more than what it was, and I damn sure wasn't about to get caught up in the "life".

The "Life" to me was dating a new dope boy every time the last one went to prison, fuckin the celebrities that come through, getting drunk every night, yapping about everybody else's business, and trying to get saved by a nigga. I saw so many girls get ran through caught up in the "life" and it happened quick too.

It's like in that environment you become a beast and a lot of chicks will do anything for money and material possessions.

Some girls come in with good intentions but completely lose themselves in the "life". I never once met a stripper who liked dancing. It's the money that motivates you to do it, so a lot of girls are in there hoping and praying to get saved by a nigga.

A lot of girls must smoke, drink, or snort just to do that shit every night. And you have some chicks that are straight lifers too, which is sad.

Lifers are dancers who have been doing it for a long time and have no plans on stopping because they don't know anything else. It's so hard for them to stop because they've built a lifestyle around their stripper income and they wouldn't be able to keep that lifestyle up working a regular job. So, you have women in their late 30's and 40's still on the pole.

Although I was making more money, there were a lot of things about the club I didn't like. For instance, the violence was at an all-time high. Security would damn near beat niggas to death if they got out of pocket. Every Sunday and Tuesday it seemed like a brawl broke out. I'm talking stools being thrown, niggas being hit in the head with bottles, niggas getting their teeth kicked out, and even a few shootings. It was just way too much for me, so I decided to stop working Sundays and Tuesdays even though they were the busiest nights.

After being there a year, I decided it was time for me to move on. I was about to transfer from my college to go to Georgia State University and I honestly considered giving up dancing all together.

I'd been doing it for two years. I had money stacked so I thought about waitressing instead.

I tried waitressing for about a month at the club I was at and realized I didn't want to take that much of a pay cut. But I also knew I didn't want to dance there anymore though. I wanted to go somewhere more lowkey and more professional. So, I jumped ship and went to a white strip club.

Working at a white strip club was like night and day, literally. It was nothing at all like the two black clubs I'd worked at before. It was more like a job, which I didn't like. You had to be there at a certain time each night, you had to work at least one slow day every week, and you had to take a breathalyzer test before leaving each night.

The crowd was diverse and totally different from my prior clubs. There were a lot of corporate executives, doctors, lawyers and dentists. The music was hard to get used to also. There was no hardcore Atlanta rap like at the black strip clubs. The closest they got to playing hip hop was T-Pain's, "Buy You A Drank". Other than that, I was dancing to rock and pop music. The major difference, though, was in the money.

Oh, I thought I was making money before, but the white club was where the real deal Holyfield money was!

Men spent money totally different at this club. There was no making it rain. Instead, you had dudes paying for dances on their *Amex* cards and it was the easiest money I've ever made.

My first night as soon as I walked out on the floor an older white gentleman called me over to the bar to dance for him I only danced about 4 songs then he asked me to go to VIP I was hesitant but decided to do it because VIP sections at this club were open and there was a security guard present. VIP was $200 an hour we went to VIP for 2 hours once we got to the back I danced a few songs then he asked me to sit down and talk, we talked for the remainder of the time back and I was fucking shocked I couldn't believe I made $400 that easily but honestly it went like that a lot.

The guys at this club were more interested in talking and getting to know you. They loved telling their personal business about work, their relationships, and everything else in between. It was both weird and profitable as fuck. I didn't have to twerk, make by butt clap, or dance until I broke a sweat either. I could just sway side to side and look pretty, I never left work tired or with sore feet. The money was too easy to make, and I very quickly racked up a cult-like customer base that came every week for me and only me.

The girls at this club were different too. There were only a handful of black girls and we all stuck together pretty much. A lot of the girls were in school, and there were some girls there with full careers like nurses and teachers who liked making the extra money. None of us hated on each other. We all helped each other make money.

I got to know a few of the girls. We would go eat at R. Thomas, which is a dope 24-hour restaurant with organic food or IHOP after work sometimes. There was never any violence between security, customers, or the girls, so I never went to work fearful of what might pop off like I did before.

I went on vacation to Miami with one of the girls from the club once. I went to work for a whole week, 6 days straight, which was something I NEVER did, but my plan was to take everything I earned that week to blow in Miami.

I made over $7,000 and went to Miami with it. I had a blast shopping, riding jet skis, and eating lobster dinners on Ocean Drive. We went to club Rolex and made it rain, and I got a butterfly tattooed on my back at 3 a.m. after partying at club Bed.

I was making more money than ever, shopping, and having a great time, but while working at the white club my relationship completely fell apart.

My boyfriend got another girl pregnant and we never really recovered after that. The girl didn't end up having the baby, but he'd crossed a major line and I just couldn't look at him the same. There was no way we could ever be together again, so we went from being in a toxic relationship to being in a toxic *situation*ship.

He started dating other people and so did I, but he was still like a moth to my flame. No matter who he was dealing with he would still be concerned with what I had going on, as if I was still his girl. He would still show up at my house, and we would always end up fucking no matter who either of us was dealing with.

I used to laugh when he would get so-called new girlfriends because all he would do is compare them to me and then call me complaining, telling me how no one else was like me. He would always say, "You ruined me; no other woman is anything like you. You always smell so good, you're the cleanest woman I know. No one else has your sense of humor, and all of these chicks get on my nerves."

The problem I had with dating was that men wanted to lock me down and wife me right away and that wasn't what I wanted. I just wanted to have fun, not be in a serious relationship.

Outside of him, I'd been known to be a runner. In the beginning of my relationship with him, I'd tried to run too but he was beyond persistent.

Men got attached to me very easily. I would have men telling me they loved me, or felt I was the one very early on and I would get so turned off by that! If a dude started getting clingy or expressing his feelings for me, I would cut him off and never speak to him again.

After working at the white club for about a year, I moved into a 3-bedroom house and purchased a new car before the age of 23. I was in school full time at Georgia State as a business major, I was making $3,000 or more per week *easily*, and I'd developed quite the shopping addiction. My spending habits were no longer as modest as they'd been before.

I was going to Lenox every Sunday. Bebe, Juicy Couture, BCBG, Gucci, and Michael Kors became my favorites! I would buy stuff just because. A lot of it I never even wore. Every time my little sisters they came over, they left with something. When I would clean out my closet, I'd let them get first dibs on everything before taking it to the Goodwill or a consignment store.

I went to the hair salon every single week, I loved pampering myself with massages, I loved eating at nice restaurants, and I loved being able to do things for my little sisters like taking them to Birthday Bash, which is a huge concert that happens every summer in Atlanta.

It felt great being young and financially free. Outside of going back in forth in my *situationship* with my ex-boyfriend, life was sweet, and it was about to get even sweeter.

One night I was up on stage when this much older guy (his hair was literally snow white) came up and put five one-hundred dollar bills in my garter and said, "Please come and see me when you get off stage."

I got off stage, went to the back to freshen up, then I walked over to his table. He was there with a friend. I danced for him the whole time they were there, which was about four hours. He gave me $1,000 and asked if I would be working the following weekend. I told him I would be.

He came back the following weekend by himself and he danced me the whole time he was there. This time, we talked a little bit more. I told him I was in school and what I was majoring in. He asked if I had kids and I told him about my son.

He told me he was an entrepreneur and owned his own tax company. After being there for a couple of hours he gave me $1,000 and left. He began coming every weekend and he would not dance anyone else but me. Every time he spent at least $1,000.

One weekend, out of nowhere He said, "You know, I don't have to come here to give you money." I asked what he meant by that and he iterated, "You're in school and you're a single mom, and I want to help you. How much are your bills every month?"

I told him and he said, "Okay, I can give you that amount every month. In fact, I can put it directly into your account and you can stop working here if you want."

Naturally, I didn't believe a guy would be willing to put in excess of $5,000 in my account every month without wanting anything in return. So, I continued dancing and decided I would let him show and prove before I made a decision about quitting.

He kept his word and not only gave me what I needed to cover my bills; he also took me on crazy shopping sprees. Like, I could go to Lenox and get whatever. I didn't even have to ask; he would ask me. I still remember the first time he asked if I felt like going shopping. I said, "Yes, I always wanna go shopping."

We got to the mall and I must've left with over 30 bags full of clothes, shoes, jewelry, and perfume. He walked slow and with a slight limp but would insist on carrying all the bags. He'd walk behind me with his hands full and the brightest smile on his face.

It got to where I shopped so much and frequented the same stores so often, I would have stores calling me every week to let me know about the newest items.

He was much older and walked slow and because Lenox is such a huge mall and I frequented so often, we made an agreement. I'd get to the mall first and go from store to store leaving everything I wanted at each register. Then I'd call him when I was about done to come meet me at the mall. When he got to the mall, he'd make his rounds to each store and pay for all the stuff I had waiting at each register.

My older sister once said this was something out of a movie. Those who knew about him couldn't believe he was doing so much for me, financially, without asking me for anything in return.

He was always respectful, and we became good friends. I learned a lot from him about entrepreneurship. He knew a lot about taxes and laws, and I was able to really soak up a lot of gems about business from him. He was never bothersome, he never asked me questions, and he never blew up my phone. Like, he knew he wasn't my man and he knew I wasn't attracted to him in any type of way. He understood we were just friends.

I went by his office a few times per month and he always gave me cash — one-hundred-dollar bills to be exact. He'd give me thousands of dollars at a time like it was nothing. I was like a big spoiled kid.

I was still dancing, but only a few times per month. I mean, I had money stacked for a rainy day, and I had a sugar daddy spoiling me rotten, but me being who I was, I still worked because I didn't want to rely on his money. The gravy train could've stopped at any moment.

After a while, the recession hit hard and the money in the club was nothing like it'd been when I first started. Making $500 a night, which was my minimum, became a struggle. I started feeling like I needed a drink just to walk in the door, the high-end clients were no longer coming in, and what was left were the broke penny-pinching dudes.

I knew it was time for me to stop when I started breaking my rules.

I'd been dancing almost 4 years and I'd never smoked, drank liquor, or dealt with a dude from the club. I briefly got involved with this lowkey D Boy that used to come in. It was fun. He took me shopping all the time, he would surprise me with gifts, and we went out to eat and partied damn near every day. He claimed to be on the outs with his wife when we initially met (which I later found out was untrue) and he went to prison shortly after, so our relationship was very short lived.

I had 2 semesters of college left and the 4-year mark for dancing was approaching. Financially, I was in a good place but knew I needed something else I could do.

One of my closest friends at the time told me about Delta Airlines hiring part-time agents. I was kind of insulted when she told me how little the pay was, but she stressed that wasn't the point. I would be able to fly for free. When she said that, my mind went Ding! Ding! Ding!!!

I continued dancing the first couple months of working at the airport. I worked at the club on weekends, went to school on Tuesdays and Thursdays, and I worked at the airport Sunday, Monday and Wednesday mornings.

Before long, the club became a complete joke. I could no longer deal with the penny-pinching low lifes that came in and going to another club was out of the question. I was over it and I knew I was at my wit's end.

I decided to downgrade from the 3-bedroom house I was living in because by now the recession was in full swing and I wanted my overhead expenses to be lower, especially since I knew the club was about to be a wrap. I still had my sugar daddy but would never put myself in a position where I was solely dependent on him for money.

On a cold winter night, I walked in, put my dance clothes on, and went out on the floor. I walked around the club one good time then sat at the bar for a few minutes looking around the club. As I sat at the bar, I said to myself, *I can't do this anymore.*

I went to the back, put my clothes on, paid my tip out, and never looked back.

That was the end of me dancing for good.

11

∞

Young Fly and Free

Life actually got better when I left the club. I had more freedom, I didn't have to work late nights or weekends anymore, I had money being put in my account every month on GP, and I could fly free!!!!

Me and my friend started at the airport together and literally used our flight benefits to go to Miami right away.

My oldest sister was living in New York at the time and I made her my travel companion, so she had flight benefits too.

I would go to New York to visit her and we'd go eat our favorite Indian restaurant in Soho. I was taking my son on trips everywhere too. To LA, New York, Vegas, and Memphis to visit family.

The first international trip I took was to Jamaica! I flew business class, which was one of the perks of being an airline employee; you got business class seats on most international flights.

Me and my sister went to Montego Bay and had a phenomenal time. We were treated like royalty from the time we stepped off our plane.

We stayed in an all-inclusive resort and had a beautiful beachfront suite. The water was clear blue and warm, and the hospitality was out of this world. For example, when we were on the way to our room, the bellhop asked if I smoked. I told him yes, but I didn't know how to roll. He said no problem and rolled 3 joints for me right then.

The food was amazing! There was a lot of tall dark Jamaican eye candy, I got my groove back (wink wink) and I could smoke weed on my balcony while watching the sun set. Yes...Jamaica was paradise.

Although I was traveling, shopping, and living financially free, there was a lot going on with my family during this time.

My father went back to prison and was sentenced to 50 years on conspiracy charges. My youngest brother was diagnosed with schizophrenia. My two-year-old niece was in and out of the hospital fighting for her life with a rare lung disease that she ultimately died from. My favorite aunt was diagnosed with AIDS, and we found out some very disturbing news about my grandfather and his pedophilia. All of this took an extreme toll on my family.

I was never good at grieving or mentally processing emotional events, so I blocked everything out. That was my way of handling things. I had to stay super busy so I wouldn't have time to think about any of it.

I couldn't allow myself to stop to think about my dad and the fact that he'd die in prison. It was just too sad for me to fathom. Since his coming home when I was in middle school, he and I had two spats in those early years. But overall, our relationship was good, and he was close with my son too.

I couldn't stop and think about my baby brother who I loved so much being schizophrenic. Me and him were so close as young kids and I couldn't believe this happened to him. At the time I couldn't understand how he lost his mind out of nowhere. He always came and got me when something was wrong, we were both Capricorns, and he was the best little brother. When we were little, I used to suck my two fingers and I had a habit of playing with ears when I did. It annoyed everyone else hut he would always let me play with his ears, it never bothered him. Every time me and my other brother fought, it was normally over me standing up for my youngest brother. Me and my youngest brother had one fight with each other our entire life, and thinking back, it was over something so stupid.

He had so much potential! He was smart, funny, very sweet… a momma's boy at times, a star athlete, fast as lighting, and strong as a bull. When he was younger, we all knew he was going to the NFL for sure. And I just couldn't understand how or why mental illness took this life altering toll on such a beautiful spirit.

And my aunt… she was so funny without even trying, she would have everybody in the room dying laughing. I loved her voice. She had a slow proper voice with a heavy LA accent. My aunt struggled with an addiction to crack cocaine and a lot of my family members assumed she got AIDS in relation to her drug addiction but none of us really knew how she got it.

I was doing everything I could to keep my mind off what was going on with my family. So, my daily schedule was pretty hectic.

I was in my last year of college taking a full load to make up for the change I'd made in my major. I'd decided to switch from Finance to Business Economics and I was going to be taking a super heavy load of classes for the entire year so I could graduate on time.

I was going to school Monday-Thursday, my son was playing Pop Warner football which took up my evenings and Saturday mornings, and I was working 3 days a week at the airport.

Around this time my eating habits got completely out of control. I ate out 2-3 times a day most days. I would eat breakfast at this cafe close to my school, eat pizza on campus for lunch, go to work at the airport and eat more fast food, then order takeout on the way home or cook a frozen heat and eat meal for dinner.

I'd been slim my whole life and I could pretty much eat whatever I wanted without gaining weight, but suddenly, I started picking up weight. I didn't have a lot of time and honestly, I was too concerned with sweating out the fresh press I got weekly so working out was out of the question.

An old friend of mine from the club had recently gotten lipo and she told me they did a post procedure where they injected the fat into her butt. So, I did my research and decided I'd do the same.

I told my sugar daddy about the procedure and he paid for it with no problem, but the joke was on me. It ended up being a complete waste of over $6000.

I got lipo but didn't really have enough fat for a fat transfer to my butt, so the second part of the procedure was an epic fail.

The lipo didn't do much either, other than leave little tiny incisions on my back and stomach. I honestly would've been better off hiring a personal trainer. But you live and you learn right???

Going into my last semester of college I decided I needed a change. I moved to a brand-new place that was much more expensive than the last, but I wanted an upgrade. Me and my ex were on the outs, we hadn't spoken or hung out in a while. Then one night he asked if he could come by and I let him.

When he got there, he spilled an entire cup of juice on my laptop and broke it. He was so apologetic, swearing he would buy me a new one. After he completely reneged and refused to replace my laptop, he refused to take accountability for it and tried to flip the script on me. So, I completely cut him off. My sugar daddy ended up buying me an even better laptop than I had before a few days later. I also decided to take a trip to Cairo, Egypt with my son for his 8th birthday.

Cairo was absolutely amazing! Me, my mother, and my son flew first class to JFK, where we met up with my sister. From there, we all flew business class from JFK to Cairo. We stayed at the Cairo Marriott in a beautiful suite. We decided before going we didn't want a touristy visit; we wanted to really get out and experience Cairo on our own.

We had a great driver named Khalid who took us around the entire week we were there. The people of Cairo showed us so much love. Everywhere we went, they told us, Welcome Home.

My son was treated like a little king. The people there were just drawn to him. I had 3 different men offer my mom camels in exchange for my hand in marriage. One man offered one million camels in exchange for me and we all died laughing like yeah right. For the rest of the day she and my sister joked about leaving me there while they cashed in on camels.

We took a carriage ride around the Nile river; we went through the slums and saw how people in real poverty lived, and I was extremely humbled. After seeing people living in clay huts with no doors, windows, or floors, seeing young children begging for food in the streets, and seeing the conditions many of the people in Cairo were living in, I realized how fortunate I'd been my entire life even when I was "poor".

We went to see The Great Pyramids of Giza and the Sphinx. We all got into a carriage together for a tour around the pyramids then we got off to ride camels. After seeing that picture on our living room wall my entire childhood, seeing the Sphinx in real life felt completely unreal.

I was so proud to be black, I was so proud to be of African descent, and I was so proud to be witnessing this in real life. I had to keep pinching myself. I was *really* there in Cairo, Egypt with my family seeing this greatness with my own eyes.

I said to my son, "See, when you learn about this in school you will be the ONLY person in your whole school who has seen it in real life."

Going to Cairo was one of the best experiences of my life!

After my return from Cairo I was a few weeks away from completing my degree in Business Economics, and right around that time I realized going into corporate America or working a desk job wasn't for me.

I thought about my entire college journey and realized I had no passion at all for econ or finance. Of all the courses I'd taken there was only one course I enjoyed, and it was about the economy of South Africa.

The professor was an older black man. He was amazing! He'd spent so much time in South Africa he could teach the course from the top of his head. I learned so much about history. I learned the truth about so many things like the diamond trade and what it did to the indigenous people of South Africa.

I learned about the colonization of Africa, and I learned about the true beauty, wealth, and size of Africa. He once said even how Africa is positioned on the globe is a lie. He pointed out how you could take every other continent and put it inside of Africa and there would still be room left. That's how massive in size it is.

We had to do a map quiz of Africa, so I had to learn every country by heart. I was enamored with this class because I was learning something that really resonated with me. We had to write a 20-page term paper that counted for half our grade. I wrote about the De Beers family and the diamond trade in South Africa, and I got a 100!

On a freezing cold December afternoon, I graduated from Georgia State University with a degree in Business Economics. All my family and closest friends were there to celebrate with me. We had breakfast at R. Thomas after the ceremony and I got my favorite banana French toast.

***

After graduation I had a huge decision to make. Prior to graduation, I planned to get my MBA, work for a company to get some experience, then start a business of my own. But I just couldn't see that for myself any longer.

Pursuing a real career at the airport was out of the question because the pay just wasn't gonna cut it for me. I was sick of college and honestly felt it'd been a waste of my time.

I got a degree in business and knew nothing about starting a business of my own. The only thing I learned was how to become an employee for someone else, it was like I learned a bunch of unimportant information I couldn't use to help me in my everyday life. So, the idea of going to grad school went down the toilet.

I decided I would go to cosmetology school instead, and boy did people think I was crazy!

Becoming a hairstylist was a childhood dream of mine. I used crayons and colored pencils to write a book about opening a salon called, "Dream Girls" when I was in elementary school. I loved playing with dolls as a kid, and I was the household hairstylist for my sisters and few of my friends.

But when I was young being a stylist was frowned upon. People felt doing hair was for the loser girls who couldn't do anything else, which is why I didn't pursue it after high school. With me being a teen mom, I didn't want the stigma associated with being a hairstylist. So, I felt I needed to go to college and get a degree in something hard to prove my intelligence to the world so I wouldn't be looked at as a dumb teen mom.

After graduating from college, I realized I wanted to do something I enjoyed, regardless of what people thought. I knew the hair industry was technology and recession proof, I knew it was a skill I could use anywhere in the world and more than anything, I wanted the freedom of working for myself. I'd been working at the airport for a while and had gotten accustomed to being a sheep— wearing a uniform, being on someone else's clock, and working less than ideal hours. I was over that. I did enjoy my flight benefits, but not enough to stay somewhere I knew I didn't belong.

I found a cosmetology school near my home with an accelerated program that could be completed within 10 months if I were to go full-time. Going full-time would mean M-F from 9am-4pm so I would not be able to do that and stay at the airport. I knew this was what I wanted to do but decided to give myself a little more time at the airport so I could travel.

The year after graduation I traveled my ass off. I went to Rio De Janeiro, Brazil and had an amazing time. Brazil was breathtakingly beautiful. I knew that from what I'd seen on TV and magazines. What I didn't know was that I'd see so many black people.

I saw men and women who looked just like me. Same skin tone, hair texture, and everything. Everywhere I went people came up to me speaking Portuguese because they assumed I was Brazilian.

The attendant at the front desk of my hotel couldn't believe I was American. She kept pointing at her face then pointing at my face saying, '*you look just like me.*'

I stayed in Ipanema. My hotel was super dope. We had a pool on the rooftop and from the rooftop you could see the whole city! I had Christ the Redeemer on one side, the Favelas on the other side, the mountains behind me, and the ocean in front.

The favelas are the settlements former slaves gathered in once slavery was abolished in Brazil. The Favelas were where all the poor people in Rio live, they have no running water or electricity in the Favelas, so they have to make a way themselves.

At night the entire mountain side would light up like a Christmas tree. I would watch from the rooftop thinking of how determined and genius they had to be to create their own electricity up there. I wanted to go to the Favelas and connect with the real people of Brazil but was warned not to by the hotel staff. Plus, the friends I went to Brazil with were not about that life, so I didn't go.

One day we were at a cafe on the beach and a group of young boys from the favelas between the ages of 8-10 ran up to our table. They were barefoot, their clothes were stained and tattered, and they were pointing at the food we were eating, asking if they could have some. They were so cute; the leader of the group reminded me of my son. The restaurant owner came out shooing the young boys away, telling them to get lost. He apologized to us for them running up to our table, but we assured him we didn't mind the young boys being there.

They ran down the street a little after being shooed away and were still pointing at our food. So, my friend said, "Fuck it, let's give them the whole plate." We had a plate of different types of grilled meat, so we gave the whole plate to them and they were ecstatic. Their little faces lit up with joy as they devoured the plate of grilled meat. We also gave them a few Brazilian *real* to put in their pockets before we left.

The beach in Brazil was like something from a movie. There were so many people on the beach you could barely see the sand. Vendors walked up and down the beach selling everything from food, coconuts, and water, to Brazilian bikinis. The water was deep blue and there were rip tide warning signs everywhere. I'd never seen a real wave like the huge ones you see surfers surfing through until I went to Brazil. The waves were gigantic! It was so cool watching the surfers go through those huge waves. There were guys playing soccer and women jogging along the beachside. Brazil is an active country. People are in action all day and night.

I drunk a lot of *caipirinha,* which is the official drink of Brazil. I ate delicious Brazilian food, and had a wonderful time watching the exotic birds from the rooftop of my hotel.

That year, I also went to The Bahamas, Mexico, LA, Vegas, New York, and Miami.

I had a guy friend I was seeing and me and my ex hadn't spoken in months. It was the longest we'd ever gone without seeing each other. I'd finally started feeling like I could really move on from him.

I was at work one day so eager to get off because I'd mistakenly left my blackberry on the kitchen counter that morning. So, I had gone all day with no phone. When I got home, I had a million missed calls and text from my ex. Thinking something was wrong, I called back immediately.

He told me he took a contracting job overseas and that he'd be headed for the Middle East in a few weeks. I congratulated him on his accomplishment. It was something he'd spoken about doing before, so I was happy for him. I honestly felt an enormous amount of relief. I felt I really could move on with my life without him swooping in like he'd done every other time.

I was at work the morning he left for the Middle East. He asked if I would see him off, so I did. After the flight took off, I walked away thinking, *Good, now let me get the fuck on with my life.* Over six years of going back and forth with him had been long enough.

I didn't have communication with him once he got overseas until I was coming back from a birthday trip. I was at the airport in San Juan, Puerto Rico headed home from the best girls' trip in life. We'd stayed in a beautiful beachfront suite overlooking the pool at our resort in San Juan. The beach was mesmerizing! The sand in San Juan wasn't white like other beaches I'd been to. It was dark brown, and the ocean was deep royal blue with waves strong enough to wipe you out.

From our resort we could walk to different cafes and nightclubs. We took a trip to Old San Juan and partied hard. We were at a salsa club one night and my oldest sister had the whole club doing the electric slide. It was epic; everybody applauded her after.

We were about go through airport security and I saw this weird number calling. I never answered numbers I didn't know, so I ignored it. A few days later I was home cleaning and I saw the number again. I ignored the call assuming it was a telemarketing company or something.

I didn't know how wrong my assumption was, but I was soon to find out.

12

∞
_____∞_____

The Ex-Factor

A few days later I was at work preparing to board a flight and I saw the mysterious number again. I ignored it and it called right back. This time I answered and the first thing I heard was, "Baby it's me don't hang up."

I told him I was about to board a flight and couldn't talk. He asked if he could call me later that evening and instead of sticking to my guns I said yes.

He called later that evening very apologetic about a lot of the damage he'd caused in the 6 plus years we were involved with each other. He kept saying, "I love you and I miss the fuck out of you."

He said he wanted to take me on a trip when he came home on his first R&R, which was the paid vacation time for contractors overseas. I was reluctant while on the phone with him, but when we got off that night, he'd accomplished his mission. His hooks were back in.

We talked or messaged just about every day for a few weeks. He let me know he planned to stay overseas for two years, but more than anything he wanted to know who I was dealing with, and he let it be known that he wanted us to be together again.

This was so fucking typical of him. Of course, he wanted me to be with him. He was so afraid of me moving on while he was gone.

I was still getting money from my sugar daddy but other than that I didn't have anyone I was interested in. Although I couldn't stand to admit it, I knew I still had feelings for him. So, although it went against my better judgement, I took him back.

We Skyped all day every day, messaged, emailed, and he wanted pics of me damn near every day. He made a collage of pics of me on his wall at work that he called his shrine.

We were on different sides of the world in different time zones. I would stay up all times of night and morning to talk to him. It felt like our beginning days when we wanted to talk to each other all the time. Our connection felt magical again.

He spoiled me to death while he was over there. He'd send me money and random gifts and we had a trip to Vegas planned when he came home for his first R&R.

His first R&R came a few months later and the trip to Vegas was the best Vegas trip I'd ever taken. It was my cousin's 30th birthday weekend so a whole bunch of us went. Me and him stayed in a huge suite at PH Towers. There were TV's in the bathroom, a huge jacuzzi in the master bedroom, a panoramic view of the whole strip, and the windows could turn into a movie projector. We had full kitchen and dining room, and a red leather sofa that stretched around the entire living room.

For four days we partied, had the best sex ever, shopped, and ate at some of the best restaurants on the strip. When we returned home to Atlanta, the fun continued. We went to the Hawks game, partied at Diamonds of Atlanta (which was the hottest strip club at the time) did more shopping, ate dinner at Capital Grille, and brunch at Pappadeaux.

Our chemistry was back on a trillion! We were like two teenaged kids and because we'd physically been away from each other for so long, the sex had elevated to a whole new level. Every time was one for the "history books".

He was home for a few weeks before going back overseas. Then it was back to Skype calls and IM's. I started cosmetology school the week after he left. Once I started school it was going to be impossible for me to stay at the airport because of my school schedule. So, I decided to quit my job.

A lot of people questioned me quitting my "good" job but working there long-term was never my goal. Yeah, the flight benefits were great, but I planned on becoming wealthy. I didn't need to stay at a low paying job for free flights. So, one Sunday afternoon I clocked out, got on the employee shuttle that took us to the parking lot, got in my car and emailed my supervisor to let him know that I would not be coming back. He emailed back and asked if I was sure. He reminded me that if I quit without notice, I wouldn't be eligible to be rehired.

I told him, "Good! I have no plans on coming back."

That was the end of me working for the airline. I could now solely focus on cosmetology school and becoming an entrepreneur.

I knew being a hairstylist wasn't what I wanted to do long term. I just wanted a way to work for myself and doing hair was something I always wanted to do. Hair extensions completely dominated the hair industry, but I'd never worn extensions and didn't know anything about how to install a weave. So, I decided natural hair would be my specialty.

At this time in my life I felt happy. I was doing something I enjoyed. I was no longer working for the man.

My relationship was in a good place. I had more time to spend with my son, and financially I was in a good place.

With me officially being back in a relationship, and this time around with us being more public because of social media, people started asking when we were getting married. It's crazy because I'd never even thought about marriage in all the years I'd been with him.

I'd never mentioned marriage to him once. He'd always been the one to call me wife or remind me of what he thought when he first saw me. I wasn't against marriage or anything, it just wasn't something I cared about. It wasn't on the top of my list and I honestly felt if I was happy with whoever I was with, I didn't need a piece of paper to validate my relationship. And none of the women I was around in my upbringing were married or in good relationships

Plus, I had taken a class on the economy of South Africa I knew the truth about diamonds, so I didn't care about a diamond ring either. So, when people would inquire about when we were getting married, I would say, "Who knows?"

He was due back for his second R&R, and we had a trip to Punta Cana, Dominican Republic planned for his birthday. I was super excited. I loved buying him gifts. He would always say, "Man, you know how to pick the best gifts." This particular year, I'd gotten him Burberry everything: shirts, boxers, and cologne. I remember my oldest sister saying out of the blue. "I know you love him, and I know you think he's the one, but he's not. I'm telling you!" She said, "Keba, you won't be able to be great with him; he's not on your level. He will clip your wings."

I couldn't believe my ears. I didn't understand why she was saying what she was saying because I'd never shared any of the real drama I'd been through with him with my family. So, I didn't know how she'd come to this conclusion about him.

My sister was like that, though, and she was always very protective of me for some reason. It was like she always saw a level of greatness in me that I couldn't see in myself. She would say things like, "You are so intelligent, but you never let people know how smart you are. Why do you sit around talking about the *Real Housewives* when you know about economics and history?"

I loved information, I was a documentary buff, and I enjoyed deep conversations. Still, being young, materialistic, completely consumed with Reality TV, and keeping up with the Joneses, the shallow meaningless conversations were what I'd been accustomed to.

I completely ignored what my sister said about my man. I felt she had no grounds for her words, so I went on preparing for my trip to Punta Cana.

Punta Cana was amazing! We stayed at a beautiful all-inclusive resort with a jacuzzi in the living room of our suite. We had breakfast in bed each morning, got couples massages, and drank more Mamajuana (which is the official drink of DR) than should be allowed.

On his birthday night, when we returned to our suite after dinner, the jacuzzi was filled with bubbles and rose petals, along with a bottle of champagne on ice waiting.

When we returned from the Dominican Republic, the celebration continued. We went to an all-white party at Compound, which was one of the hottest clubs in Atlanta. We went shopping at Lenox and Phipps Plaza, and hit all our favorite restaurants.

A few days before it was time for him to leave, he said he wanted to have a big dinner at the Cheesecake Factory. He wanted to invite everyone, all our family and friends. I said cool since I thought that would be a great way to end his birthday trip home.

We went to Cheesecake Factory on a Saturday night and although we had a reservation there was still a wait because our party was so large. As we were waiting more and more people started showing up. I'm like, *damn, he really did want everyone to be here. This is going to be fun.*

Our table was upstairs on the deck. We were all laughing and talking over dinner and the next thing I know he stood up and started tapping his glass. I thought he was about to thank everybody for coming out, then I listened closer to what he was saying.

He said, "I love you and we've been through a lot these last 7 years. You've been my girl..." Everything went blank after that until I heard him say, "I don't want you to be my girl anymore, I want you to be my wife."

Everyone started pulling their phones out. Clearly, they all knew this engagement was going down. He got on one knee, pulled out a diamond ring, and said those four words that most women crave to hear their whole life.

"Will you marry me?"

I said, "Yes!"

He was nervous as shit! I could feel him trembling. He put the ring on the wrong finger, and we all laughed as he slid the ring on the correct finger. We embraced each other, kissed, and everyone went crazy clapping, and congratulating us. And, of course, everyone wanted to see the ring.

I was on Cloud 9 and in shock at the same time. I wanted to know how my mom and everyone else kept this a secret. I wasn't even the bride type, but once that ring hit my finger it was like I drank the Kool-Aid and snapped right into it.

I would be the first of my siblings to get married and have a wedding.

13

∞

Bride 2 Be

Everyone was super excited and ready to jump into wedding planning mode with me.

Although I was excited, me and him both agreed to have a modest wedding. We weren't about to go into debt or break the bank for a one-day celebration. We chose the first Saturday in November of the following year as our wedding date. A few days after our engagement he went back overseas, and I got busy planning.

Planning was simple. I didn't have to hire anyone. I did my research and found an all-inclusive venue. I went to view the venue with my oldest sister, who was my maid of honor. Although she was skeptical about him, she was supportive and excited about the wedding too.

We were able to taste the food, taste the cake, and meet the florist. I was pleased with what the package included and the price, so I decided on the venue right then. I sent him pics of the venue and the price and he was pleased with it too.

We decided our wedding decor would have a fall color theme, there would be lots of earth tones with splashes of champagne gold, and I chose bouquets of calla lilies and hydrangeas for our center pieces.

We chose a sleek 3-tiered strawberry cake with fresh strawberries inside covered with butter cream icing for our cake. My fiancé wanted to ensure two things were on point: the music and the bar.

Our playlist was insane! All hip-hop and oldies, and we chose our favorite mixed drink, Coconut Ciroc and Pineapple juice, as our signature cocktail for the wedding.

After we were a few months into wedding planning he was due for another R&R trip, but this time he didn't want to come home. He wanted to fly me to Dubai for a week instead.

I was so excited! Dubai was one of the places I had on my list while working at the airport, but never made it. I knew the flight was 15 hours straight, so I was prepared with books and my neck pillow. My sister and cousin dropped me at the airport, and I made my way to the UAE.

My flight got to Dubai got in a little before his, so I had to wait for him in the airport. I still remember how bright his face lit up when he saw me.

We went to eat and then went straight to our hotel room and made up for lost time. The sex was explosive! Dubai was too much fun. We went to Jumeirah beach and the Dubai mall. I was in awe of how gigantic this mall was and at how much money was being spent. I saw women wrapped in their hijabs coming out of Louis Vuitton and Gucci with handfuls of shopping bags.

In Dubai, wealth is an understatement. You see Bentleys and Rolls Royce's like they're nothing. The cab we rode around in for the week was a Lexus, the clocks on the walls at the airport and mall were Rolex clocks. The city is swathed in wealth and opulence, and we experienced it all.

We visited the Burj Khalifa, which is the tallest building in the world, we went on a dessert safari, we rode dirt bikes and camels. We had so much fun. We really got out and enjoyed Dubai. We walked around the jewelry district, where you have dudes trying to whisk you off to private apartments where they sell all the knock off designer shit and fake jewelry.

We talked to the Black locals about life in Dubai. One night, we got a section at this hip-hop club and turned up, just the two of us smoking hookah and drinking Rose. Afterwards, we went back to the room for one of those history book nights.

When I returned from Dubai, it was time to get back into wedding planning mode. I was almost finished with school also so I was busy trying to learn as much as I could about the business side of being a stylist too.

I found my dress at *Brides by Demetrios,* a bridal shop in Buckhead, Atlanta. I'd initially come in for a dress I'd seen in a magazine. It was a sleek, one shoulder gown with a vintage feel. I tried the dress on, and I liked it. So did my mom, my aunt, and my bridesmaids.

Then the bridal clerk who was helping us said, "I have a gown that I think will look really beautiful on your frame. Do you mind if I bring it to you to try on?"

I said, "Sure."

She brought me an eggshell white fit and flare gown with beautiful embroidery and beading at the top, along with a corseted back.

I tried the dress on. When I looked in the mirror, this dress was stunning. It had a completely different feel than the dress I'd come in for. When I walked out, everyone was floored. This was the one, for real. My mom offered to buy my dress as her wedding gift to me, so I had my dress, we had everything with the venue set, and we decided on Negril, Jamaica for our honeymoon.

I was excited for him to come home on his next R&R so he could see the venue. However, on this trip home, to my surprise, he had other plans.

Randomly he said, "Fuck it, let's go get married now." I said, "Ok."

I mean, it wasn't a huge deal. We were due to get married later in the year anyway. So, we went to the courthouse in our county and got married, just the two of us.

After our nuptials, we went and got something to eat and he kept saying 'wife' after every word he said to me while we were talking. I was dying laughing! We agreed we would keep us being married a secret.

Nothing felt different after we went to the courthouse and got married, but I did start thinking, like, *Damn, we just got married. That's a real legal document.*

Up until that point I hadn't thought about the fact that we'd never discussed finances, cultural beliefs, short-term goals, long-term goals, or any of that. We were so caught up planning the wedding and doing all the surface level stuff that we never once stopped and had a real conversation about building a solid foundation as a married couple. In fact, in all the years I'd been with him we never talked about anything of substance.

The few times I attempted to talk to him about money because I felt he was spending too much, he would assure me that he had it under control and that he had more than enough stacked.

It was as if we both assumed everything in our marriage would just come together since we'd been eating good, going out, traveling, and having great sex for almost 8 years. And we'd practically lived together, right? I mean, he was at my house 4-5 nights a week when we dated. That had to count for something. I figured I knew what living with him would be like. I felt marriage would be the same exact thing as being boyfriend and girlfriend with just different titles and living under the same roof 24/7. No big deal, right?

I did know one thing for sure, though, and that was I didn't want to ever get back into that toxic tit for tat cycle we'd been in while we dated. I told him I did not have the energy to do that shit for a lifetime. He assured me that his slate was clean, and he had nothing going on outside of our now marriage.

I'd already stopped communication with my sugar daddy before we got engaged. I didn't tell him I was getting married, though, I just told him I had a lot going on and would be out of touch. So, we hadn't talked in months.

So, I went into my marriage hopeful, feeling like we'd moved past the childishness, dishonesty, and possessiveness. Boy was I wrong.

***

My maid of honor oversaw planning my bachelorette weekend and she chose New Orleans as our destination to have a weekend of partying and fun before the big day.

My fiancé was home from overseas for good by this time and he and his crew were going to Miami for his bachelor's weekend.

The wedding was two weeks away and I wasn't getting cold feet. It was too late for cold feet; we were already married, but for some reason what my sister said about him the year before kept replaying in my head. A part of me felt like this was all a huge mistake but I couldn't say that out loud. I mean, the wedding was paid for, we had people coming in from out of town, and he was the love of my life, my soulmate. I had to be tripping. There was no way this could all be a mistake. Or could it?

111

I couldn't get those thoughts out of my mind. It was like I couldn't visualize or see myself with him for a lifetime, or at all in a real way, but I didn't have the guts to verbalize what I was feeling.

So, I asked for a sign. I'd recently gotten into watching *The Secret* and learning about the Law of Attraction so I felt if I asked for a sign I would find out if this really was a big mistake or not. That sign came sooner than I expected.

We were getting dressed so he could drop me at the airport. My flight was leaving for New Orleans a day before his flight was leaving for Miami. He was about to jump in the shower, and I was putting the last few items in my bag when I realized my iPad was at the bottom.

"Shit!" I said.

He said, "What's wrong?"

I said, "I wanted to check in for my flight on my iPad and I don't feel like digging it out from the bottom of my bag."

He said, "Babe, just use my laptop."

So, as I'm checking in for my flight, an email popped across the screen. I saw enough of the message to know it was from a female he was dealing with intimately.

This was so typical of him. He was never the type of cheater that humiliated you publicly or had drama coming to you from other females. He always answered the phone, he was always where he was supposed to be, he always returned messages, he never missed a beat, and he kept the women he dealt with in line. Never once did a chick call or message me over the years of being with him.

I'd literally seen messages where he told a chick, "You already know what it is. I'm not leaving my girl, so you gone play your role or not?"

112

He always dealt with women who were okay with being side chicks. He could be on the phone with me right in bed with another woman. He was that type of cheater. It was his careless mistakes that always got him caught. I honestly wasn't even surprised. I'd been doing this dance with dude for over 8 years, so I sought to see the extent of his infidelity this time.

Since I'd already gotten a good glimpse of the email, I went to his inbox and read the entire message. This one was from one of the many chicks he'd been fucking with during our entire engagement, and apparently, she was in her feelings about him getting married.

I immediately went off on him. He jumped out the shower and tried to defend himself, but he couldn't. He was caught red-handed.

He begged me not to leave, he begged me not to call the wedding off. He swore he would change his number, get off social media, and go to counseling after the wedding.

I wanted to say, "Fuck it all! Get your shit and get out." But the wedding was two weeks away. People had flights booked, we'd already paid for everything, and we had a trip to Negril booked.

I couldn't *not* go through with it. So, I agreed to stay and go through with everything, but in my mind, I already knew what time it was. I wasn't gonna do this toxic dance with his ass.

So, I put on my happy soon-to-be bride face and went to New Orleans with my crew. We stayed in a house not far from Bourbon Street. There were 20 of us total in NOLA that weekend. We partied hard, smoked a lot of weed, drank a lot of liquor, and ate a hell of a lot of beignets.

We were walking near Bourbon street one afternoon and the basketball player, Anthony Davis, passed us in a car. He had his driver circle back, and he got out of the car and

113

invited us all to lunch. So, we all went. After being at the restaurant for a while a well-known public political figure joined us. He let it be known as soon as he sat down that he was interested in me – whether I was the bride to be or not. He was wealthy *and* handsome. I was tempted to oblige in some risqué behavior out of sheer spite for my soon-to-be —no wait, my already husband —but decided it wasn't worth it. No one knew it, but the whole time I was in NOLA I was full of regret, secretly plotting on how I was going to leave him after we got back from our honeymoon.

When we returned from our bachelor/bachelorette weekend I never brought him cheating back up. I just went on like everything was cool. We had our rehearsal and rehearsal dinner the following weekend and then it was time for the big day.

On the day of our wedding the weather was perfect. It was a sunny fall day, no humidity in the air, and still warm enough to go outside without a jacket.

I had a car come pick myself and the bridal party up from my mom's. I'd gone to her house for pre-wedding brunch. We arrived at the venue and my glam squad got started on my bridesmaids first. I did a walkthrough of the venue with the coordinator. It was everything I'd wanted it to be.

The colors were perfect, my centerpieces looked unreal, and the cake was flawless. I was so pleased with how everything came out. I talked, laughed, and drank champagne in the back while getting ready, and for a moment, I forgot about our drama. I allowed myself to get wrapped up in this wedding fairytale.

Since my father was in prison, my brother was going to be walking me down the aisle. My sisters were my bridesmaids and my son was a Jr. groomsman. I walked down the aisle to Larry Graham's, "Just Be My Lady". He'd played that song for me on our first date.

I wanted our reception to feel like a night out at the club, so we came in to, "I Got a Feeling" by the Black Eyed Peas. Then, we had our first dance to the O'Jay's, "Forever Mine" and from there the DJ played Jay-Z, Kanye, Future, and Migos all night.

We made our grand exit through a tunnel of jumbo sparklers held by our wedding guests and we went to the Presidential suite we had booked for the night after. We were due to leave for Negril the following morning.

The wedding was so fun, but it all went by so fast it was like a blur. While on the flight to Negril I had the chance to look at all the pics being sent to my phone and posted on social media.

Negril was amazing! The water was warm and turquoise blue, the sand was soft as powder, the vibe was chill and laid back, and the food was outstanding.

We had a beachfront suite and a half ounce of weed to blow. I didn't dwell on anything negative, I just enjoyed being there with him. We got couples massages, rode jet skis, stuffed our faces with Jamaican food, and fucked nonstop. It was a wonderful week in paradise, indeed, but as soon as we touched down back home the fairytale would be over and reality was about to set in.

He changed his number when we got back but refused to go to counseling like he said he would. I never believed in arguing back and forth or bringing up the same shit over and over so after he refused, I didn't bring it back up.

It was just more fuel on my fire to leave him. I soon realized leaving was going to be harder than I thought though. We were married now; for me to walk away would mean taking legal action and then everyone would be in my business. I was a super private person when it came to what went on in my relationship.

I was the first of my siblings to be married. My mom was so proud, everyone thought we were the perfect couple. I couldn't let them all down. Plus, I was in my late twenties, everyone in my circle was married, engaged, or in a serious relationship. I didn't want to be the only single divorcee.

The more I thought about it the more I realized how attached I was to the word *wife* and how I attached I felt to the diamond ring on my finger. I never cared about marriage or any of that stuff before, but now I was part of the married club and I didn't want to give that up.

To make matters worse, I wasn't financially in a place where I could leave him and be okay. I'd just started building my clientele as a stylist, so the money wasn't consistent yet. I'd cut communication with my sugar daddy, I'd damn near depleted my savings preparing for the wedding, and for the first time in my adult life, I didn't have anything to fall back on.

My husband was the breadwinner and for the months leading up to the wedding I wasn't really working at all. I was used to a certain lifestyle, I'd never struggled financially since the age of 19, and I was not about to start. I did not want my lifestyle to change. I did not want to live on any level lower than what I'd been accustomed to. I mean, cheating wasn't the end of the world to me, and at my core I knew I never expected for him to really be faithful anyway. So, I psyched myself out and decided that it would be in my best interest to stay.

I never mentioned him cheating to anyone, I never mentioned leaving to anyone; I just put on a happy new bride face everywhere I went. We hung out with friends, went out on weekends, went to family get-togethers, and continued as usual. No one ever suspected anything, but on the inside, I was a volcano laying dormant.

14

∞

_____ _____

The Snowstorm from Hell

It was almost time for my birthday, and I decided to have dinner at New York Prime with my closest family and friends then we went to a lounge to party after. Little did I know, that would be the last time we all ever partied like that together.

About a week after my birthday the city of Atlanta had the biggest snowstorm we'd ever seen. It was later coined *Snowmageddon* because it was a complete disaster.

We had the typical snowstorm warnings, but no one took them seriously. Most schools didn't even close. Everyone assumed it would be the same ole same ole, a few flurries that don't stick and we all go on with our day. How wrong we were.

This storm hit and escalated so fast no one was prepared for what came next. Luckily, I lived in a county who'd closed school for the day. My son had a doctor's appointment that afternoon around 12pm, and as we were leaving, there were flurries coming down. I decided to go to the store and get a few things because you never know. So, we went to the grocery store and by the time we got home it was full-on snowing hard. The snow accumulated lightning fast.

Once I got in, I called my friend because she worked kind of far from where she lived, and I wanted to make sure she was home safe. She told me she had just gotten off and the snow was so bad she couldn't even get out of the parking lot at her job. She said traffic was terrible and there were wrecked cars and people in disarray everywhere.

I cut on the news and saw the whole city was a complete mess. The expressways were in a grid lock, traffic wasn't moving at all. A lot of the streets were completely frozen over, people had to abandon their cars, and walk. There were school buses full of children stuck all over the place, many of them were stranded overnight. People had to walk 10-12 hours just to get home after abandoning their cars. A lot of people slept in their cars overnight. All the hotels in the city were sold out so the hotels allowed people to sleep in the lobby.

Stores were completely sold out of food. It was like some end of the world shit. I was grateful to have been home that day, I was grateful that I'd followed my gut and went to the store, and I was grateful my son wasn't stranded on a school bus like so many kids were that day.

The next day was followed by even more snow. They ended up closing school for the whole week and the entire city was officially under a State of Emergency.

The upside was that it was so beautiful outside it was like a winter wonderland. My son wanted to go outside and have a snowball fight. So, we all put on our coats and shoes and went outside. There was a hill on the side of our house, so we went up top to have our snowball fight.

We'd been out maybe ten minutes. We'd just started having fun when my husband jokingly nudged me. When he nudged me, I lost my balance and slid down the hill. Because of how I was standing when he nudged me, I landed back on my left leg when I hit the bottom of the hill. Immediately, I heard something snap like a twig.

I knew something was wrong because when I tried to get up, I couldn't feel my foot and I couldn't stand on it. My husband and my son ran down to help me up but even with them supporting me, I couldn't stand on my left foot. So, my husband picked me up and took me in the house.

I took my shoes and my socks off and my left ankle looked a little swollen, so I thought I sprained it, but I kept saying I heard something snap so it might be broken.

The streets were frozen over. The whole city of Atlanta was under a state of emergency, everyone was instructed to stay off the streets, so I decided to just monitor it. I elevated it to see how it felt in a few hours. I didn't want to risk driving to the ER if it wasn't serious.

After about an hour, the swelling had gone from 0-100. My ankle looked like a grapefruit was sitting on the side of it. My mom happened to call, and I told her about my ankle. I took a pic and sent it to her. She called immediately.

She said, "That's more than a sprain! You need to go to the emergency room. Call the paramedics so you can go straight to the back."

We called the paramedics. Me and my son got in the ambulance and my husband followed behind in his car. They immediately gave me some pain meds and performed X-rays. Then, we had to wait about 3 hours. They came back and said my fibula was fractured, and because of the way it was fractured, I would need to have surgery. For that, I would have to go see an orthopedic surgeon once the roads cleared up. They put me in a temporary cast and gave me a prescription for pain. I'd never broken a bone, gotten stitches, or been seriously injured, so this was weird for me.

I immediately thought about my job. Things were just starting to roll. How was I going to do hair with a broken ankle? I didn't want to freak out too much. I wanted to wait and see what the surgeon had to say.

I was in my temporary cast for about two weeks. Once the roads cleared, I was able to get an appointment with the surgeon. The first thing the surgeon told me was that I would never be able to wear heels again, which completely devastated me. I had a whole collection of designer heels that I loved. He twisted the knife further and told me that not only was it broken, but a part of the bone had slid out of place and I would have to get a metal plate and 3 screws inserted in my ankle during surgery. The whole process would take approximately 3 months to completely heal from and would require physical therapy after. He advised me to stay in bed as much as possible until I had the staples removed due to the nature of the injury.

After hearing that news, I felt like my whole life had fallen apart. I was on my ass, literally.

So now I'm in a marriage I know I didn't want to be in, I couldn't work so I had no money coming in, and I had to lay in bed all day. This was my worst nightmare come true.

Besides the pain I was in, I didn't know what I was going to do for money since I couldn't work. As if things couldn't get worse, in so many words my husband informed me that he had severely mismanaged his money and didn't have as much saved as he led me to believe.

It'd been over a year since I'd spoken to my sugar daddy and I didn't want to randomly call and ask for money. That wasn't my style. I was so mad at myself for having a closet full of designer shit, but not having enough money in my bank account to leave my marriage or pay my damn bills. I felt completely stuck.

I was so angry at my husband. I blamed him for everything. This was all his fault! He fucked our marriage up, he pushed me down the hill. Because of him, I'd never be able to wear my favorite Jimmy Choo pumps again. On top of everything, this nigga had spent thousands upon thousands of dollars on designer clothes, belts, and shoes while overseas and now he had me stressing over how our bills were going to get paid. Even before my sugar daddy I could always pay my bills I was never stressing over rent or utilities. After all the money we spent on trips, the wedding, partying, and eating out, I couldn't believe the position we were in.

I could still remember how mad he would get or how fast he would shut a conversation down and remind me it was his money when I would try to tell him he was spending too much. I was full of regret for taking him back in the first place, then being dumb enough to marry him.

Amidst my anger, what I couldn't possibly have known at the time was that everything I was going through was preparing me for a radical metamorphosis.

Part 3:
Spinning the Chrysalis (Maturing Adult)

15

∞

Change is Inevitable

"How strange that the nature of life is change, yet the nature of human beings is to resist change. And how ironic that the difficult times we fear might ruin us are the very ones that can break us open and help us blossom into who we were meant to be." -Elizabeth Lesser

A few nights after my surgery I had a breakdown in my bathroom. I couldn't understand how my life had turned into such a big mess. I looked at myself in the mirror and didn't recognize my reflection. That night I realized two things: 1) I was miserable as fuck, and 2) I had no clue as to who I really was.

It was like I'd been on this rollercoaster ride of shopping, traveling, partying, and being caught in a toxic relationship with the same man for almost a decade and I'd never stopped to think about the meaning of life in a real way. But the rollercoaster ride was over, and I was 29 years old with no real purpose for my life.

That night I had a complete breakdown, I cried to myself until I got a headache and couldn't cry anymore. Before going to bed I asked whoever was out there listening to help me, I didn't ask for money, I didn't ask for a better husband, I simply asked for clarity and guidance.

In the middle of the night something so bizarre happened. A voice woke me out of my sleep and said, *Now is time!* I looked around the room like WTF? My husband was still sound asleep, so I sat up in my bed for a moment trying to figure out what this meant, and although I was a little freaked out, I managed to get back to sleep after a while.

The morning after my breakdown I woke up thinking about my past. I thought about everything I'd experienced since high school, and out of nowhere, a paper I wrote my first semester of college popped into my mind. This was my first English class and we were asked to choose a controversial topic to write a 3-page paper about. I chose to write about obesity and how it disproportionately affected African Americans. I got an A on the paper and the professor said he rarely gave Freshmen A's on their initial papers, but he was so intrigued by this topic because he'd never had anyone write about it.

After randomly thinking about that paper I was compelled to do more research on health and nutrition. I started by watching every documentary I could on Netflix. I watched *Food Inc, Farmageddon, Tapped, Forks Over Knives,* and *The Beautiful Truth.* I ordered tons of nutrition books from Amazon. I ordered "The Pleasure Trap", "The China Study", and "Food Seduction", just to name a few. I watched lectures on YouTube and filled notepads with notes on healing the mind and body through nutrition.

It felt as if my whole life was falling from under me and it was completely out of my control. I needed a way to control some aspect of what was happening in my life. We were still fresh into the New Year and living healthier had been a goal of mine for a while. Although I was on bed rest, I thought to myself I still want to live a healthier lifestyle and I *can* completely control what I put in my body, so I decided that day to completely change my eating habits.

After making this decision I was compelled to go into my kitchen and throw away all the junk and processed food in there. So, all the cereal, Pop Tarts, Capri Suns, chips, cookies, and frozen meals had to go. From there I decided to go on a 90-day clean eating journey which meant no processed food, no refined sugar, no fast food, and I also stopped eating meat cold turkey. I would be eating wild caught fish, lots of leafy greens, fresh fruit, and drinking a lot of water.

Before starting my clean eating journey, I used to have headaches almost every day. To my surprise, after just two weeks of eating clean, my headaches were completely gone.

Prior to eating clean I would have random acne outbreaks. Now, suddenly, my skin was clear. I would feel sluggish and need to take naps every day. Suddenly, I had the energy of a child. I couldn't believe how much better I felt only after a few weeks.

By the time I hit the 60-day mark, I'd lost 20lbs and weight loss wasn't even my goal. I just wanted to be healthier, but I was amazed at the added perks. I couldn't believe I'd lost 20 lbs. with no exercise, just by changing what I was putting into my body. That was when I realized the power of good nutrition.

During this time, I learned so much about how the foods you eat affect you mentally, physically, and spiritually. I learned about the connection between the gut and brain, and why good gut health was the key to good mental health.

When I went in for a follow up visit with the orthopedic surgeon, he said I was the first patient to lose weight with a broken ankle. He said all his other patients used it as an opportunity to pig out in bed.

I was loving the benefits of eating clean. I had more energy, my skin was clear, I was excited about everything I was learning, and more than anything, I had more mental clarity. It was like the lights had been off all my life and suddenly they were on. My mind felt clear, and I was looking at everything differently.

My husband was against the whole lifestyle change. He didn't want to change the way he ate, he didn't like that I was spending so much time researching and watching documentaries, and he didn't want me to change what I was eating either.

He would say, "Can you just go back to what you used to do?" He was very vocal about his disappointment in how slim I'd gotten too.

I thought maybe if we did this together as a family it could possibly save our marriage. So, I wanted to share the journey with him and although he'd lost weight too and improved his health some, he was still against it.

I started sharing my journey on social media, posting what I was juicing each day. I would post health tips, and I would post about the documentaries I'd seen. I woke up each morning with excitement and looked forward to learning more about health and wellness every day.

He, on the other hand, was in the process of starting a small business with friends. So, he would get up and leave each morning, and come back later in the afternoon. I would spend the day researching.

I learned about healing chronic ailments such as asthma, arthritis, high blood pressure, fibroids, and high cholesterol through nutrition. I learned about meal prepping and eating the right foods for the body I desired. Working out had never really been my thing, but with me eating healthier and feeling so good, I knew once my ankle was healed, I wanted to get the fitness aspect under control too.

It was almost time for me to have the staples removed from my ankle, which meant I'd be back on my feet soon. I was excited about getting out, driving, and most of all, going to the gym. I decided I would join a gym close to my house and that I'd hire a personal trainer to help me build the body I'd been envisioning.

I started watching *Super Soul Sunday* every week and looking at YouTube videos from different thought leaders which made me want to learn more about energy, universal laws, and spirituality. I researched everything I could about meditation, energy, and the law of attraction. I would try to talk to my husband about it, but he was like a brick wall. He didn't believe in that kind of stuff he thought it was hooky he said meditation went against what he believed in. He was originally from a small town and when it came to health, spirituality, and anything of substance his mind was even smaller.

He was only interested in shallow conversations and I'd gotten to where I didn't want to talk about Reality TV, celebrity gossip, or watch fights on WSHH. I wanted to have more meaningful conversations. Eventually it got to where we didn't talk much at all and for the first time ever, I didn't have that strong sexual attraction to him. It was like it died once I saw how small his mind was. His jokes were no longer funny to me, it was like we were on two totally different pages.

He even went to talk to my mom about our relationship, which was something I never *ever* did. I never discussed any of my personal business. As an adult I got to where I had a decent relationship with her, but I never shared my business with her. I only talked to her about very surface level stuff. She was known for gossiping behind everyone's back, spreading rumors, and telling your business to anyone who would listen. She called me and said, "He is very upset about all the changes you're making. He said he wishes you could just be the old you."

I remember thinking, *how can someone be mad at me bettering myself and trying to help them better themselves?* I knew right at that very moment what my sister said about him was true. He didn't want me to elevate, he wanted me to stay small with him so we could continue doing the same damn thing we'd been doing for damn near a decade.

I recall him even saying once: "I already know if you blow up and start making a lot of money you're not even gonna want to be with me anymore."

I know a huge part of his insecurities stemmed from the thought of me becoming more successful than him and then leaving him for a man with more than he had.

As I was elevating on my journey of better health and spiritual awakening, I was constantly sharing information on social media, and with my family and friends. I wanted everyone to get into taking better care of themselves.

A family friend had mentioned a book to me about two years prior and I told him back then I didn't think I was ready to read that one yet. So, this book randomly popped into my mind and I decided to google it. After reading the reviews, I immediately ordered it. The book was called, "Ask and It Is Given".

This book was like music to my ears. It helped me realize so much about myself, so much about life, and I felt so empowered after reading it. When I finished the last page, I immediately went back to page 1 and read the book over. After the second reading, I read it again from cover to cover. After the third reading, I read it once more. After reading that book four times in a row from cover to cover, I knew that if I really wanted to live the life I desired to live, I needed to leave my husband ASAP.

It was like the more I tapped into my own health and well-being, the clearer my thoughts and vision were. I saw our relationship for exactly what it had been for the past 9 years. We'd been fucking, partying, and going out to eat for almost a decade, but when it was all said and done, our relationship didn't have a drop of substance. We had never, in 9 plus years, even had a deep conversation about anything. We didn't have anything in common when it came to higher goals in life and he did not have the desire to expand his intellect. I realized he didn't know what his purpose was in life nor was he interested in finding out. His vision for what he wanted in life was the complete opposite of mine. The only thing we had keeping us together was good sex and that was no longer worth being with him for.

He was not open to changing anything about himself, he wasn't open to learning anything about spiritual growth, or financial growth, and he wasn't open to going to counseling — which by this time I wanted him to go for his temper, not for what happened before our wedding. I was past that. We couldn't have a conversation about anything without it turning into a heated argument.

Once I got my staples removed and could get around on my own, I felt so much relief. I was ready to get back to work and I was ready to hit the gym. I'd lost over 20lbs while recovering from my injury, all from eating clean. My plan moving forward was to hire a trainer and gain the 20lbs I lost back with lean muscle.

I found a trainer that specialized in what I was looking for and when I shared the news with my husband, all hell broke loose. He went off! He forbade me to go back to that gym, forbade me to work with a male trainer, and suggested I go to a female-only gym. I couldn't believe my ears. Who did he think I was, some little kid or something asking my dad for permission?

I never understood how a habitual lying, cheating ass dude thought he could have the nerve to control where I was working out or anything else I was doing.

I continued going to the same gym and decided I would still hire the trainer. My husband would do things like take my keys when I tried to leave for the gym. He even came up there once and demanded I leave while I was in the middle of my workout.

Once I was fully recovered from my injury, it was like his insecurities and possessiveness kicked in like never before. He was so concerned with what I may do to get back at him for cheating. He knew from our past how spiteful I could be and the one get-back he found out about while we were together, he never got over. Even with all the cheating and bullshit he pulled (and it was a lot I could write a whole book on just that) he would still try to hold this one incident over my head. So now that my ankle was healed and I was in the gym getting fine he was worried that I would find a better man to leave him for.

I would try to talk to him about goals and planning for the future and he would be so negative. My plans were always to become a self-made millionaire. I wasn't sure how, but I knew it was what I desired. I had a picture of my vision board as my screensaver on my phone.

I remember him saying to me one day. "Your dreams are too big, man. Like, you want things that aren't even possible. I just want a regular job and a nice house."

See, me, I didn't want anything regular. I wanted to start a business of my own, become extremely wealthy, have homes around the world, and give back to my community.

My 90-day clean eating journey was almost over but I wasn't stopping. I'd lost 20lbs, completely got rid of my migraines, I no longer needed my three asthma inhalers, I was sleeping like a baby, and my hair was healthier than ever. Because I'd been sharing my journey on social media, by now I had people reaching out to me for coaching and I was invited to do a few speaking engagements too.

I felt better than I'd ever felt before. People were actually coming to me for help and for the first time I felt like I had a purpose, that I was on this earth to do something bigger than me.

I was also ready to get back to work. I found a new salon and was busy building my clientele. I'd gone to a class before hosted by a world-renowned stylist and he gave us a tip on building clientele. He said if you give out 60 cards a day for 90 days you can build a very solid clientele fast. So, I would do my hair every week then go to the mall. Normally, I'd have women ask me about my hair and from there I'd give them a card. Or if I saw a woman with natural hair, I'd give her a card. I did this every single week. Sometimes my ankle would get so swollen from walking around different malls all day, but I still did it and before long I had a steady flow of clients coming in each week. Once I had money coming in that's when I put my plan to leave my husband back in motion.

Tension was high between us. We barely talked to each other, we weren't having sex at all, and we hadn't been out since before I broke my ankle. I was completely wrapped up in work and studying everything I could about nutrition.

Despite this tense energy in our relationship, baby talk would still come up from time to time. I remember calling my closest friend once the baby talk started. I posed the question: Would it be horrible of me to get on birth control without telling him? Hearing myself ask that question (and the response she gave me) assured my gut feeling of knowing divorce would be inevitable — and it would have to happen sooner than later.

My mom had a big family vacation to Panama City Beach planned, and of course, she invited us. I told her me and my son would be coming but my husband would be staying home. I told her he had something up with the business he was starting and couldn't come, but truth be told, I didn't want him to come. The beach was exactly what I needed. Being on the water, being away from him, and just feeling like I could breathe for the first time in a long time felt so good.

We stayed in a 3-bedroom beachfront condo for the week and every morning I got up early to watch the sun rise. I had a lot of time to think. No one knew what was going on in my marriage. Everyone thought everything was all good and I was so sick of pretending. It was too much pressure.

I don't know what it was, but something made me say the *D* word out loud one day while we were all sitting on the beach.

We were talking about where we'd take our family vacation the following year and my mom mentioned my husband's name in her list of people that would be there.

I said, "I'm pretty sure I'll be divorced by next year."

Everyone paused and kind of looked at me funny. I don't think they knew how serious I was.

When I got back from Panama City Beach, he told me things with starting the business hadn't gone as planned and that basically we were dead broke. There was no money left. He'd been online trying to find a job for weeks and nothing came through. We had a family friend in the electrical business, and he was making decent money with the company he was working for. He said he could pull some strings and get my husband hired, but it would require him working out of town.

He took the job and started work right away. He had to head out of town immediately. Prior to him leaving we'd discussed getting a bigger place once our lease ended. The lease would be up soon, and I knew I did not want to move into a new place with him. My plan was to leave him for good, I didn't want to fuss or argue about it either, so I knew leaving while he was gone for work would be my best bet.

By now my mom and everyone else knew about my plan to divorce him and everyone was begging me to stay and begging me to try counseling first. It was too late for all that. He'd already shown me exactly who he was, and counseling wasn't going to change my mind about leaving him. I couldn't stay with a possessive, insecure, small minded, habitual cheating ass man with no standards in the kind of women he cheated with, that wanted to hinder me elevating.

When I told him I was leaving I don't think he really took me seriously. He knew I was broke, and he knew I was very prideful. He kept asking me where I would go because he knew I wasn't going to move back in with my mom. He thought I would stay with him just to save face in front of my family and friends, but I was beyond that. I didn't give a fuck about what anyone would say or think about me. No one was walking in my shoes and no one was living my life. I was doing what felt best to me.

After one year since the day we went to the courthouse and got married, and 7 months since we walked down the aisle, with no money saved and no type of security net whatsoever, I walked away from my marriage for good.

16

∞

Emotional Wreck

Since I didn't have any money, I sold all the designer clothes, bags, and shoes I had. I got rid of all my furniture, sold my appliances and electronics, I sold my wedding dress, wedding shoes, and my ring. Then I moved in with my mom briefly.

I knew leaving him was the right choice, but I was not at all prepared for the emotional rollercoaster I'd be on as I went through the divorce process.

Once I left, it took a few weeks to kick in but when it kicked in, it kicked in hard. I was a mess! I blocked my work calendar and didn't take clients for weeks. I was crying all day every day. I could be in the car and hear a song that reminded me of him and break down.

It felt like I was grieving a death. Because I wasn't one to express emotions in front of everyone, I would silently cry to myself when people were home but when I was there by myself, I would cry and wail out loud uncontrollably.

It had been a total of 10 years and I couldn't help but think back on all the good times. It was hard to accept never celebrating another birthday or going on another vacation with him. Just a year ago I was on Cloud 9, so excited to be marrying the love of my life. How had it come to this?

I knew him like the back of my hand. I knew he'd find another woman ASAP. He wasn't strong enough emotionally to go through this by himself. I'd heard through family that he was already dating someone else, so I unfollowed him on every social media platform and informed my family and friends not to report anything he was doing back to me. I didn't want to know his business. We were not together anymore, and I wasn't going to add insult to injury by trying to keep up with what he had going on.

It was very tough. I couldn't talk to my family and friends. They were all biased. They all liked my husband so much and wanted us to work it out. I needed someone I could vent to with no judgement or biased opinions, who wouldn't gossip about me or slander me, so I decided to go to counseling.

Going to see a therapist was something I was very skeptical about. I was very private, and it was very hard for me to open up about my feelings, but I couldn't make it through the day without breaking down into uncontrollable sobbing and I didn't want my son to keep seeing me in that condition.

I went to therapy twice a week for a little over 3 months, and it helped me tremendously. The first few sessions I could barely even get my words out because I was crying uncontrollably but after a while, I could get through my sessions without crying at all.

The therapist talked to me about energy and vibration. She reminded me that my soon to be ex-husband had already moved on and it may seem as if he was winning right now but that's the worst thing you could do after a breakup.

She said, "You can only attract from where you're vibrating at and right now your energy is very low because you are going through a traumatic time. So, if you were to get out and date right now you would only be able to attract another low vibrating person."

She added that this is why rebound relationships rarely last.

I found what she said profound. I knew the best thing for me was to focus on myself, and to really give myself time to grieve over my relationship so I could heal emotionally. This was easier said than done, though.

When you spend 10 years with someone, you're constantly reminded of that person. I would smell certain scents and think about him. I'd see something funny and think of him, every song, every movie, everything around me reminded me of him.

I couldn't sleep at night, I didn't have an appetite a lot of days, and I felt an enormous amount of shame and self-pity. I was no longer a wife; I was a broke soon-to-be divorcee sleeping on my mom's couch.

Some days just getting off the couch was a challenge, but I knew in my heart, I'd made the right decision. I knew the pain I was feeling was temporary and I'd come out better on the other side.

The gym became my second source of therapy. I was going to the gym 6 days a week. The gym was the only place I could go and completely zone out. I could put my headphones in and for 90 minutes I didn't have to think about anything that was going on in my personal life.

So, I looked forward to going every morning. I worked out with my personal trainer 4 times per week and I would pick his brain about fitness during every session.

One day, he commented that none of his other clients asked questions. "You really have a knack for this," he said. "I think you should get certified."

But I had too much going on. I was just getting back on my feet at the salon and although health and fitness was a huge part of my life now, I didn't really have time to focus on turning it into a business.

Outside of working out, reading really helped me while I was going through my divorce. I read this book called, "Broken Open", and another called, "When Things Fall Apart" by Pema Chodron. Both really helped me accept my divorce and where I was in life.

I went to the courthouse and got the paperwork I needed to fill out for my divorce but decided I'd wait until after my birthday to officially file. I had a girls' trip to Aruba planned and I was super excited.

Me and my soon to be ex hadn't spoken in weeks. In fact, I had him blocked on everything. My phone, social media, and email, so he couldn't contact me at all. This dude had a whole girlfriend, which I found out about through someone else, and was still crying, begging, and trying to reconcile with me.

I was disgusted with his nerve and felt I had nothing else to say to him. I just wanted to serve him with the papers after my trip so I could be done with it and move on.

My mom had a huge party for me at her house a few days before leaving for Aruba. After the party at my mom's we went to a club to continue partying. My ex got in touch with someone at the club, and by them not knowing I had blocked him and wanted no communication with him, they told him where we were.

I'm in the club dancing, laughing and having a good time. Next thing I know, I see my ex walking toward our section. I was never one to cause a scene in public, so I played it cool. When he walked up, he spoke to everyone then asked if we could talk over to the side.

He wanted to know why I had him blocked, and why I refused to talk to him.

He said, "You know what you're doing. You know you're in complete control of this whole situation and you're ignoring me on purpose. You know that drives me crazy."

The club was about to close and everyone was headed to the parking lot. I'd left my car at my mom's and rode with my cousin and that's who I planned to ride back with. When we got outside, he grabbed my arm and asked if he could please take me to my car. I knew I should've said no, but against my better judgement and not wanting to risk him showing out in front of everyone, I agreed.

The moment I got in his car I knew it was a mistake. He had this look in his eye. He started asking me why I left him, why was I doing this to him? He was crying and driving fast as shit. I told him he was scaring me. He ignored me and started bringing up all kinds of old shit that happened between us before we got married. He started accusing me of all kinds of shit. It was like he wanted a reason to get mad at me.

We were both crying and yelling at each other, and the next thing I know, he punched me dead in my mouth. He hit me so hard I didn't really feel it, but blood started gushing out of my mouth. I couldn't believe he fucking hit me! I pulled the car mirror down and saw that my front tooth was pushed all the way back and two of my bottom teeth were chipped. I went berserk!!! I started slapping and punching him in the head and face while he was driving over 80 miles an hour on the expressway. He almost crashed his BMW into the median.

When we got to my mom's, the yelling and screaming continued. He was crying uncontrollably and repeatedly mumbling, "I can't believe I hit you, I'm so sorry, I hate myself, I fucked everything up. It's all my fault."

I was trying to get out of the car and he was saying please don't get out.

Then he pulled his gun out and said, "Fuck it, I'm 'bout to just end all of this shit."

In that moment I had an out of body experience. We had crossed a very dangerous line and I had a vision of how terribly wrong this could go. I stopped yelling. I told him I loved him, I told him I forgave him for hitting me. I gave him a kiss and told him to give me the gun.

He gave me the gun and got out of the car. He rang the doorbell, my little sister answered, and he went inside. I put his gun in the passenger seat and I got in my car and left.

About a month prior, I'd left my moms and moved with a friend so I could have more privacy while saving for a new place and that's where I went after leaving my mom's house that night.

The next morning, I woke up and it looked as if I'd been run over by a Mack truck. I was due to leave for Aruba the following day. How was I going to explain my lip?

I hopped online and found natural remedies for a swollen lip, and I was able to push my front tooth back in place. I didn't tell anyone about what happened, but I couldn't get it out of my mind.

In all the years I'd been with him he'd never hit me. Yeah, he'd broken a phone or two of mine, and punched a hole or two in a wall, but I never thought he'd put his hands on me like that. I was so sad for him and for myself. He could've killed us both the night before. From the moment I got in his car, I knew he wasn't in his right mind. It was like he was possessed. That night, I learned how dangerous love can really be when it's toxic.

The following morning, I left for Aruba. I never mentioned the incident to anyone.

I stared out of the window in deep thought for most of the flight. I was so grateful to be alive. I would be in Aruba

140

for 5 days and before returning, I planned on really letting everything go.

I wanted to forgive my ex for everything, I wanted to let go of my marriage gracefully with no anger and no resentment. I wanted to leave my marriage behind without having any bitterness about men.

It was something so captivating about Aruba. I instantly fell in love. Aruba was the first place I'd been to where I could see myself living. The beach was breathtaking, the resort we stayed at had a private beach with flamingos walking around and iguanas basking in the sun. The food in Aruba was so fresh and delicious. We went horseback riding along the coastline, I enjoyed being at peace taking in the beauty of the turquoise blue water as it hit the huge rocks and boulders along the coast.

The day of our departure from Aruba we all wanted to go back and get one more glimpse of the beach. On that last trip to the beach I felt such a lightness in my heart. I'd cried my last tear over him; I'd accepted that we'd never be together again, and I forgave him for everything. Now, I was ready to go home and file for my divorce.

Filing the divorce papers was easy. We didn't own property together, I didn't want any money from him, and I hadn't even legally changed my name. So once the papers were filed it was a matter of waiting for the final divorce decree.

In the midst of me filing for divorce I was really trying to turn my passion for health and fitness into a business. I'd been getting more and more people reaching out to me for health coaching and I was trying to figure out the best way to market the business.

My mom told me about a friend of a friend of hers who'd written a book about business and she had a copy of the book. After reading the book I wanted to meet the author to get some tips about ramping up my health and fitness business.

I met the friend shortly after at a dinner at my mom's. He was very knowledgeable about business, indeed, primarily online business. He gave me my first introduction into digital marketing, and he also let it be known he was attracted to me.

We talked for a few weeks and he gave me a lot of good insight on the direction I should take my business in. He was a nice guy, he was very tall and physically attractive, but it was his mind and entrepreneurial spirit that I really liked.

We hit it off right away. We could talk about everything from health, entrepreneurship, spirituality, and books but it was very short lived. I was still in the middle of my divorce, and he wanted more than I was ready to give. He was a great guy but not the right guy for me. However, I was so grateful for meeting him because in the brief time we dated, I learned more from him than I'd learned in the 10-year relationship I had with my ex.

My divorce was finalized shortly after and I was happy that we were able to end everything on a decent note. We talked and saw each other a few times after and it was all love. But I never once regretted my divorce or considered taking him back afterward.

After my divorce I had a new level of confidence in myself. I trusted myself on a higher level too, and I knew, moving forward that I could leave any relationship no matter who it was with if I wasn't happy. That was a great feeling.

Now that the divorce was over, I wanted to focus on myself, my goals, and taking my health to a new level.

I never wanted to be toxic in a relationship again and I had certain non-negotiables for any man I would consider dating in the future.

So, I made a list of qualities I wanted in a man. I wrote them all down and sealed them in an envelope. I also established some higher goals I wanted to reach for myself. I'd recently read, "The Science of Getting Rich" by Wallace D. Wattles, and "You Were Born Rich" by Bob Proctor. From the age of 8 I'd told myself I would become a self-made millionaire. I didn't know how; I just knew I would. So, I wrote myself a letter manifesting my first million, put it in an envelope, and sealed it.

Prior to this point, I'd been vegetarian, working out 5-6 days per week, really building the body of my dreams and developing extreme discipline. I wanted to level up even more with my discipline. I felt if I could master what I was putting in my body I could master anything. So, I went vegan.

The majority of what I ate was already plant-based before going vegan, but once I made the switch over to being 100% plant-based, my mind opened even more. I had even more energy, I felt even better, and I never got sick.

I was focused, feeling better than ever, and I had a trip to LA to visit family planned. One day out of the blue, to my surprise, my sugar daddy called and asked if he could take me to lunch. It had been over a year and a half since I'd seen or spoken to him.

When I met him for lunch, I could see his health had really taken a turn for the worst. I asked about his health and learned he had a host of chronic ailments he was suffering from, the main being heart disease. I shared a lot of the information I had about nutrition with him and he was very receptive to it. We caught up on life. I told him about the salon, my upcoming trip to LA, and the health and fitness business. He was very proud of me for stepping out on faith doing my own thing. I never told him about me getting married or divorced though.

He asked how I was doing financially. I told him I'd stayed with a friend a few months prior so I could save up and that I'd just moved into a place of my own. He asked why I didn't call him before, and I simply shrugged my shoulders. He instructed me to follow him to his office so he could give me some change. He gave me $3000 and said it was just a little something to get me back on my feet.

He said, "When you get back from LA let's discuss what you're going to need for the health and fitness business."

That would be my last time seeing or speaking to him. While I was in LA, he died from a massive heart attack. I found out when I returned.

I didn't know how to feel about his death. I wasn't really sad, and I didn't cry at all. More than anything, I felt grateful and blessed to have known him. He'd looked out for me and did more for me than anyone else I'd ever known. I'd been able to gracefully leave the club and live financially secure for years because of him and that was something I'd never forget.

17

∞

Parenting Is Hard

Things in my life were still shaky when it came to money. Ever since my divorce I'd still not been able to get back anywhere near where I'd been before financially. I was used to having savings, buying what I wanted for myself and my son from the store, and living in a nice home. As a single mother I'd always been okay with raising my son on my own. When he was younger, I was financially secure even before meeting my sugar daddy and I had a lot of support from my family, so it was easy.

Now, he was in middle school and going through puberty. His behavior got worse and he became very rambunctious. He started lying about everything and getting into trouble at school and it caused me a lot of stress.

My son had a hard time adjusting after the divorce. He'd never seen me struggle and he was used to having name brand clothes, getting the shoes he wanted, and playing sports. Now, I could no longer afford the things I used to do for my son. And I was determined to make it as an entrepreneur, so I refused to get a job even when things got super tight. I knew exactly how he felt so I empathized with him. I thought back to my middle school years when I was in the same predicament with my mom. The difference with me was I always put my son's needs before mine. I would've never told my son it was his responsibility to buy his own school clothes at that age.

With my son it was even worse though because he felt entitled to it. He had been wearing name brand clothes and shoes his whole life, playing sports, and getting whatever he wanted, and it was me that created this spoiled, materialistic teenaged kid. So, I couldn't be upset with him or expect for him to understand our circumstances. In addition to my son's behavior, I wasn't happy with where I was living either, but it was what I could afford at the time. We had a roof over our head, food in the refrigerator, Wi-Fi and cable. I was able to pay my bills, but shopping and pampering myself at the spa and doing extra stuff with my son was out the door.

I was no longer wearing designer bags and shoes either. I switched my whole style. After breaking my ankle, I could no longer wear heels and between selling stuff and the changes with my weight I didn't have much left to work with. So, I wore workout clothes and athletic gear with sneakers every day.

Athletic apparel was cheap and comfortable, and I could wear my workout clothes to the gym and to work. So, I was very low key, I kept my expenses low, my car was paid off, and I didn't have any credit card debt.

I think all the sudden changes had a major impact on my son's behavior. I felt as if I could no longer get through to him. He needed a strong male figure that could give him guidance about things I wasn't equipped to give him guidance on, but there wasn't one there.

It's funny how the universe always sends us exactly what we're asking for even when we don't realize we're asking for it.

I'd gotten a good steady flow of natural hair clients coming to the salon every week, but I knew from the beginning hair wasn't something I saw myself doing long term. By now I wanted to fully focus on growing my health and fitness business. I loved being able to help people in a meaningful way.

Even at the salon I was always talking about health and wellness to my clients. When I had a client in the chair we didn't gossip. Instead, I would be educating them about what they should eat for healthier, stronger hair. And I would also encourage my clients to stop wearing weave so much so they could embrace their natural hair. I helped a lot of my clients move completely away from hair extensions.

A lot of my hair clients became my health coaching clients. That's how I really started making money with the health business in the beginning. By word of mouth and social media, I started picking up more health clients for personal training and meal plans, but I knew I really wanted to start an online health and fitness business. I hadn't forgotten about what I'd learned from the digital marketer I'd briefly dated earlier that year.

A childhood friend of mine mentioned running into some of our friends from our old neighborhood in Riverdale at an event. She said they had a multimedia company and were doing some dope things on social media. They had a page with over a million followers. She was into health and fitness too and thought they could give us some insight on growing our businesses.

She invited me to come with her to their office. We'd all known each other since elementary school but I hadn't seen them in a while, so I told her to make sure they were okay with me coming. I didn't just want to pop up. She said it was cool, so we went, and it was great catching up with everybody. We talked about old times, laughed, showed each other pics of our kids, and then we talked about business.

147

The man in charge was a childhood friend of mine I'd met when I was in third grade. He was part of the neighborhood crew in Riverdale when we were outside vandalizing houses and trying to build a clubhouse. He'd been my boyfriend for a few weeks when we were in elementary and was the first boy I kissed. He was tall and skinny as a kid, but as a man he'd gotten big... really big. He really liked what me and my friend had going on as far as business. He expressed needing help with getting his health together.

So, we talked more about business and what we were trying to accomplish, and this dude was fucking brilliant. He knew so much about growing businesses on social media. He'd started a sketch comedy page and grown it to a million followers organically within 8 months. He gave us ideas right on the spot about creating content, and doing what he called, "sweeping the royal court" on social media. He was also managing some of the hottest upcoming comedians like DC Young Fly, Emmanuel Hudson, and a few other rising stars. I'd always known him for being more into music. I knew he'd managed Young Thug in the beginning of his career, and I knew he made music too, so I was blown away by what they were doing with comedy. We chopped it up for a few hours, then left so we could beat rush hour traffic. Before leaving he invited me and my friend to a comedy show they had coming up at Center Stage, a popular theater in Atlanta.

In the weeks leading up to the show we texted a few times and I remember my sister saying, "I think he likes you."

I said, "No way." We'd been cool since we were kids. I've seen him several times as an adult and he'd never once tried to talk to me, so I didn't think anything of it.

Me and my friend went to the comedy show a few weeks later and it was just what I needed. I'd been under so much stress since my divorce, it was great having a night just to laugh. The show was so well put together. It was amazing! I was so proud of them.

After the show, we went to their afterparty at a lounge nearby. He walked into the afterparty with a date but stayed at the table me and my friend were sitting at the whole night.

As I was about to leave, he called me over to an empty room in the club and asked if I had plans for the weekend. I told him I had no plans, other than work. He asked if I wanted to go to the BET Hip-Hop Awards with him and I agreed. At this point, I'm like, maybe my sister was right, but he still hadn't directly tried to holla at me.

My youngest sister got word I was going and begged me to ask for another ticket so she could go too. He was able to get her a ticket, so she came with me, and we had a ball. It was my first time getting dolled up in a long time. I wore an all-black midi dress with the back out and I kinda sorta wore a pair of nude heels. Since I couldn't wear heels, I did what girls in Miami do — I wore flats until we got to the entrance, then I put my heels on. I could walk a short distance and we were sitting the whole time, so it was cool.

Rich Homie Quan, Future, and Diddy performed, and we went to TI's restaurant, Scales 925, after the show. After dinner, my little sister was convinced.

"He definitely likes you," she said. "He's a nice guy and I like y'all together."

After dinner he told me how he felt.

"I've loved you since we were kids, but I never thought I'd get a chance," he said. "You are a dream girl to me."

I was definitely over my ex-husband and in a good space as far as dating, but he wasn't my type physically at all. Plus, we were childhood friends. That's a no-no. You're not supposed to date friends, but how could I say no to someone who basically poured their heart out to me? Then, I thought about the list I'd made earlier in the year with the qualities a man had to have for me to date them.

Although he wasn't physically what I'd been used to, he had so many of the other important qualities. He was ambitious, an entrepreneur, brilliant, a good dad, and hungry. That was very attractive to me.

So, although he was someone I never in a million years saw myself with, I obliged him when he asked me if I would be his girlfriend. He was familiar, he already knew my family, he felt safe, he was like a cozy blanket on a cold winter night and that was what I needed at the time.

We were together pretty much every day after the awards, and because we already knew each other, our relationship moved fast. He wanted to be with me all day every day, I went everywhere with him.

My boyfriend and his brother were in grind mode, building their multimedia empire so they always had a lot going on. The energy at their condo was so exciting. There were cameras, sound equipment, and backdrops set up everywhere, along with people in and out of costumes recording skits.

My son used to love going over to their condo with me because he would see his favorite comedians from *Wild N Out* and social media over there.

He and my son got along very well in the beginning, the chemistry was very organic, and he would give my son money and get cool stuff for him. He bought my son a hoverboard for his birthday and had his favorite comedians, DC Young Fly and Nav Greene, come through to surprise him.

After we'd been dating for a few months my apartment got broken into. Luckily, he was with me the night I got home and saw my back door kicked in. After filing a report, I was like, there's no way I'm ever sleeping here again; I have to move.

Me and my son went to his place that night. I got online searching for a new apartment to move to and he suggested a better solution.

He said, "Y'all should just move here. You're right around the corner from your job, right across the street from the gym, and your son can go to a new school."

He knew about the trouble my son had been getting into, and that my son had recently been expelled from the school he was attending. He said since we were both in grind mode it doesn't make sense for you to go out and create another set of bills. He said you should just stay here and stack up.

Although we'd grown up together and things were going well with us dating, it still felt way too soon to move in with him, but I was stuck between a rock and a hard place. I knew my son needed to go to a new school and I was scared to live by myself. My peace of mind was gone after having my door kicked in. So, I thought about it for a few days and although I was very hesitant, internally, I agreed to move in.

Everything was cool in the beginning of our relationship. He jumped right into healthy living. He wanted to lose a significant amount of weight and he was very receptive to clean eating and adapting a plant-based lifestyle. The condo we lived in was right across the street from LA Fitness and we worked out together 5 days a week. He loved taking me everywhere with him. I'd be on movie sets with him, at the studio, meetings, the barbershop, the club, and social events.

He had a great sense of humor. He was professional but street at the same time, which I liked, and we got along good. I'd never dated a man like him before. You didn't have to tell him what to do. He just knew and I loved that. He was a great lover and was very romantic. He would send flowers and edible arrangements to me at the salon. He would take my car and get it washed without me asking, and if I just in plain conversion mentioned something I wanted – even if I was planning on getting it myself, he would get it for me. We went out damn near every day. He had genuine love for my son, and he supported my ambition and everything I was trying to accomplish with my business.

Dating him was fun. I had experiences with him I'd never had before. We were going to red carpet events in the city, listening parties, comedy shows, award shows, and he was looking better than ever. With him changing his lifestyle, he lost over 50 lbs. within the first couple of months of us dating and everywhere we went people complimented him on how good he looked.

There *was* a huge downside though (you knew that was coming right?) He was very insecure, and he had a lot of jealous and possessive traits. After going through what I went through with my ex I'd changed my perspective on a lot of things when it came to relationships. I'd healed and matured in a lot of ways. I wasn't a jealous or insecure woman and I didn't want to be in a toxic relationship.

I was very secure and confident in who I was as a woman, I wasn't the jealous type at all. I believed in committed relationships but with a level of freedom. I wasn't for having a man control me or make me feel inferior in a relationship. I was more of a free spirit living in the grey area of life, you know, more of a maverick. Meanwhile he saw things in black and white and believed in most societal norms and traditions.

And that's where we clashed. He would swear every dude was trying to talk to me. When we went to events if he saw someone talking to me — even if they were just saying hi, he would drill me about it as soon as we got in the car.

He would say things like, "Why was that nigga in your face so long?" Or, "Damn that nigga just couldn't stop looking at you, could he?"

I would just shrug him off, but it got worse.

He would say things about what I wore if he felt too many dudes were looking at me. He paid attention to who liked what on my Instagram page, and he would make comments like, "All these niggas want you, but I have you."

He never said anything to the guys either; his issues with his insecurities were always addressed to me as if they were my fault.

He even suggested we both change our numbers, give each other the passcodes to each other phones, and access to each other's social media. My response? Absolutely not! I didn't need to do all of that in a relationship and I knew that wasn't a sign of love. That was a sign of control and I wasn't going for it.

I used to remind him, "You can't date the girl you think every dude wants, then be mad at her when dudes want her."

He traveled for work a lot and had to be around women all the time with the business he was in and I never tripped about anything. So, I didn't understand why he was concerned. We lived together and did everything together. He had no reason to worry about another dude.

I think he was still insecure about his size and he was overly concerned about what other people thought, and I wasn't. A few people did question why I was with him. Some felt I could do better, but I wasn't concerned about what anyone else was saying. I was attracted to him because of who he was and what he stood for and that was all that mattered to me.

I had a few people suggest I was with him because he had "money". People used to love to try me with that gold-digging shit, but gold digging was never me. A gold digger is a woman who preys on men with money in hopes of manipulating them with sex, a baby, or a relationship in exchange for monetary gain. I never did that. I just happened to attract men with money, but I was never willing to fuck with someone just because of what they had, and I always had my own shit going on too. Plus, he wasn't even rich; he was on the way up. He was still in grind mode. If I was a gold digger I damn sure would've chosen someone who was already wealthy.

Aside from his jealousy and him being concerned with what everyone else was saying, our relationship was cool. We had great chemistry, and we were friends above all, so we talked about everything.

After dating for about a year, his daughters came for summer break and ended up staying. So, we all moved from the condo to a bigger place. With his daughters being there full time, things majorly shifted in our relationship. Things felt way more serious once we moved. For one, my son was in high school and he was not receptive at all to another dude telling him what to do, so there was a lot of tension between them. Then he had a lot of drama with the mother of his daughters. I'd never dated a guy with kids, so this was all new to me and it was a bit too much.

She lived in another state and was always respectful in my presence, and the girls liked me a lot, but there was constant drama between him and her. I really stayed out of it. Drama is something I don't do at all, but my name was always in it. Her anger was mainly toward him because he was with me and not with her and she was very bothered by my existence.

She would send him text and emails slandering me. He would always show them to me, and I was never bothered by them. I never mentioned or brought his baby moms up not one time in our relationship. Any time her name came up it was because of him. I knew her anger wasn't really with me. Shit, she didn't know me.

I wasn't used to drama when it came to baby mammas and baby daddies. Me and my son's father didn't have drama. When I was married, my son's father and my husband coached my son's basketball team together. All the parents thought it was so odd. One mom even asked me once "girl how did you pull that off"? Truth be told, the two of them had both helped me move once. They would both be at my son's birthday parties, they would both be at events at my mom's house, and it was never a problem.

My mom was the realist ever when it came to coparenting. She had children by 3 different men and there was never drama with any of them. She would have dinners, parties, and events and all her exes would be there with their current wives and everybody got along. So, I had that same mindset. I knew you could have kids with someone and be in a relationship with someone else and there be no drama.

By now, I'm no longer working at a salon. I still had a few clients I'd do home visits for, but for the most part I was making money with my health and wellness business. I was making money online with different digital products I created, and I had a meal prep service. Still, I was very far from where I wanted to be though.

He was traveling more than ever for work so I would be home with the girls and my son. When he was home, I'd go with him to different events, parties, and he liked for me to go with him to meetings. I enjoyed going too. I used to like seeing him handle business.

After a while it was like I fell into this housewife role. I was completely wrapped up in his world. Everything we did for the most part, each day revolved around him and what he had going and having two additional children in the house was a lot of work. So, I'd work on my business when there was time left. I was okay with that at first because I understood what he was trying to accomplish.

But the drama with his baby moms continued to get worse. He started having drama with his family too, and somehow, I'd become the center of all this drama. My name was all in it and none of it had anything to do with me. They were beefing over shit that happened way before I even came into the picture, but I had somehow become the scapegoat for their issues.

That's when it hit me. I realized I wasn't living my life at all. I was in his world and none of this was what I'd envisioned for myself.

Not saying that it was all bad because it wasn't. It just wasn't what I wanted, and I wasn't a drama person. I literally had no drama in my life when we started dating and somehow, I ended up in the center of drama that had nothing to do with me.

I decided I needed to get back laser focused on myself and the higher goals I'd set before he and I started dating. I started going to my own events and surrounding myself with other entrepreneurs. I was also into motivational speaking so I was going to Toastmasters, and I joined a business coaching program so I could learn more about online business.

When I started doing my own thing his jealous and insecure traits kicked into high gear. He was always accusing me of doing something and at the time I'd never stepped out on him, not even once, even though he'd been accusing me of shit since we first started dating. It was very annoying constantly having to defend myself.

He started taking things much further when it came to his jealousy and insecurities. He would make up whole narratives to see if he could catch me in a lie and it never worked. We had cameras in our house and when he was out of town he would watch the cameras, not for robbers, but to keep track of what I was doing.

He would literally call and say, "Why are you dressed up? Where are you going and who are you going with?"

He was out of town once and I stayed over my closest friend's one night after having too much wine and he messaged her on IG to make sure I was there. It was shit like this that drove me crazy because he literally had no reason to be so insecure.

I used to warn him that he was going to turn me all the way the fuck off to the point of no return. Or drive me to say fuck it and cheat, and when that happened, it was gonna be a wrap!

He was so insecure it got to the point where other people would be like, "Damn he's tripping." For whatever reason he always felt justified in his accusations and instead of checking himself about why he was so insecure and jealous, he would try to do reverse psychology and blame me, which never worked.

He would try to make me feel bad about having different beliefs about relationships than him. If I didn't post him on my IG page, he would feel some type of way and ask me to post him or ask why I hadn't posted him in a while. There would be days when he just had an attitude with me all day without me knowing why. Then I'd find out it was about something petty like a comment somebody made on IG or something else meaningless like that.

Again, he was worried about what other people thought and I wasn't. I didn't need my relationship to be validated by social media. One day, I deleted all the posts of him, and he got really upset. My page was used primarily for business and I no longer wanted my relationship highlighted on the page. I explained to him that I deleted every single picture that wasn't related to my business including pictures of my

157

son, close friends, and other family members so it wasn't a personal attack on him, but he still got mad anyway.

He also wore his heart on his sleeve, and I did not. So, if I didn't react a certain way, or say the right thing he would take it as me not caring.

A lot of times he thought I was cold and heartless, but I wasn't. I was more so brutally honest. He'd mentioned the desire to marry me very early on in our relationship and although I knew it wasn't something I wanted, I played along. We even went to Tiffany's to look at rings once, but I knew he wasn't someone I could marry, and I wasn't going to make the same mistake again.

He used to call me a sociopath all the time. I think it was because I didn't nag him, I never attempted to go through his phones, and I never bitched when he went out of town, or when he was around other women. I gave him room to do his thing. I wasn't the type to bitch or nag. I thought that would be something he appreciated, given the nature of his business, but it was like a Catch-22. My lack of nagging made him feel even more insecure.

***

We were in Chicago for New Year's Eve. I remember telling him while we were in bed New Year's Day that if things with his baby mama drama didn't come to a halt, and if he didn't check his jealousy and insecurities it was going to be over.

Things continued to get worse with his baby mom's. It was all too much. It wasn't what I signed up for. He was traveling more so his girls were at the house with me and I felt his baby mom's had a lot of nerve coming out of her neck about me when I was doing homework, fixing hair, and cooking dinner for her kids. I told him my tolerance for her

158

disrespect was done and that if she came for me once more via email or text, I was gonna speak my whole entire mind to her. Wouldn't you know, like clockwork, she messaged him some disrespectful shit about me out of the blue and he made the mistake of forwarding me the message. I slipped right back into my vicious ways of cutting people completely down with my words and I didn't spare her anything. I let her have it all!

I remember him calling me after seeing that message. He said, "Oh My God! That text, I can't believe you said all of that."

A few weeks later his daughters were headed back to live with their mother, and we discussed going our separate ways. I let him know I did not think we were compatible. He was too jealous and insecure, and the drama with his family and baby mom's was way too much for me. I could see the drama was going to be an ongoing issue. That wasn't something I was willing to deal with any longer.

Amidst the drama with his BM, I found out about some slick shit he did too. So, with me knowing we were on the way out as a couple, and with me no longer being attracted to him in that way, the floodgates were opened, and I got my creep on. Yep, I sure did!

He said he would start looking for a new place. We remained cordial with each other, but he started sleeping on the couch and we were more like roommates.

The end was inevitable.

18

∞

_____

Getting' Back to Me

During our relationship unraveling, my dad called from prison and told me he had a parole hearing coming up and he wanted to know if I could make it. I was shocked because my dad had been sentenced to 50 years. I didn't think him being paroled would even be possible.

My dad had been in prison for 10 years, but this 10-year bid was much different than the first. With him being gone this time I was an adult so I could go visit on my own which I would do from time to time with my son. And at the same time this go round there was a level of resentment like I did this my whole childhood, I'm not doing this shit the rest of my life I hated going to visit him in prison and everything that revolved around him being in prison. But I would still put money on his account, order him shoes, send him pictures, cards, and make sure he got his yearly package every December full of his favorite foods.

My dad was diagnosed with multiple sclerosis right before going to prison on his second bid, and he was using bee sting therapy, making dietary changes, and using other natural remedies to manage his illness before going in.

When he went to prison, he never got any type of treatment or medication for his condition. MS is a degenerative illness that can cause permanent paralysis if not treated properly. Each time I went to visit him during those 10 years he looked progressively worse. He looked 100% healthy when he went in. Now, he walked with a limp so bad he needed a cane, and his left hand was deformed. He couldn't use it at all anymore.

I'd accepted the fact that my dad would die in prison. By now I was much deeper into spirituality. So, I knew in my spirit that if the universe had aligned for my dad to have a hearing after having the book thrown at him, he had to be coming home, but I was still nervous.

About a month later, it was time for the hearing. I asked my closest friend to take the drive with me to Tennessee for support and we listened to Les Brown and other motivational speakers the whole ride. I wanted my energy to be good and I wanted my vibration to be high for the hearing.

We stayed in a hotel near the prison and the next morning my uncle came to pick me up. He and I headed to the prison for my dad's parole hearing. I had major butterflies when we pulled up. I hated the sight of prisons; I'd been going to them my whole life.

The barbed wire fences, the guard towers, the sterile almost hospital-like smell of the lobby, the buzzing sound of the gates as they opened and closed, and the loud sound of the heavy metal doors closing… I hated all that shit.

We got to the waiting area and there were about 20 men waiting for their hearing. All of them were black, but all the decision makers in the hearing room were white. I thought to myself these men don't stand a chance with all these white people in the room.

Sure enough, every single man that went in before my dad was denied parole. When it was my dad's turn, they escorted him into the room where he sat in the center and me and my uncle sat in chairs over to the side of the room.

I hadn't seen my dad in a while and he looked terrible. His health had declined so much since my last visit with him. There were 4 guards, a clerk, and a man behind a desk on an overhead projector. He was the one to make the final decision.

I just started praying in my mind for a miracle. My uncle spoke first on my dad's behalf, then I spoke. I got very emotional when I spoke. I spoke about the decline in his health and what I'd be able to do to help him if he were released. I could see in my dad's eyes that he was on the brink of death. He wouldn't live much longer if he wasn't released.

After I finished speaking, they took a minute to review my dad's records. Then the guy on the projector announced his decision.

He said, "I am approving your parole. The process will start immediately; you can expect to be home in the next 30-45 days."

I was so happy I was laughing and crying at the same time. I went to give my dad a hug and the Devil of a guard wouldn't even let me hug my dad.

He said, "NO! Inmates can't have physical contact unless it's during visiting hours."

That's the justice system for you. A man can't even give his daughter a hug after being approved for parole. Ain't that a bitch?

There was one black female guard in the room when the other guards left. She said, "Darling, you can give your dad a hug."

So, I gave him a long hard hug.

As soon as I got to the car, I sent a mass text to everyone in my family letting them know he was coming home. When I returned from Tennessee, I got everything prepared for my dad's arrival.

A month later we picked my dad up from the Greyhound station. As we were driving through the city he was amazed at how much everything changed. The whole city was being gentrified, there were high rise condos being built on every other corner, a lot of major films were being made in Atlanta, and Atlanta had the hip-hop scene on lock too. So, everything was much more alive than 10 years prior.

He got settled in and it was great having my dad stay with me. My son was happy to have his grandpa home. My dad would play his oldies all day. Earth Wind and Fire, Teddy Pendergrass, and The Dramatics were his favorites.

However, I did have a few things to get off my chest with my dad. We had one spat with each other. I spoke my mind and he spoke his, and we never had another argument for the rest of the time we lived together.

With my dad being there the energy in the house was much better. I think my soon to be ex felt we would be able to work things out. We were getting along better, the drama had ceased, and he was helping me a lot more with my health and wellness business.

He eventually stopped bringing up moving out and he stopped sleeping on the couch and started back sleeping in the room with me. Things were going well for him with his business too. He was about to close a major deal and he was anticipating everything he was going to do once everything with the deal came through.

He started back mentioning us getting married, he mentioned buying me the luxury car I wanted at the time, and he mentioned us getting a new house, and his daughters coming back to live for good.

It sounded good and I know most women would've jumped at the opportunity, but he just wasn't the guy for me and that wasn't the life I wanted. I knew telling him that I still did not see a future with him although we'd been getting along better would be hurtful, but me going along with something I knew I didn't genuinely want would've been worse.

So, I told him I still wanted to break up. He didn't take it well at all so things got tense between us again and he started back sleeping on the couch. I knew I'd be responsible for all the bills when he finally moved so I started looking for something I could do to supplement my income.

I was still doing hair here and there and although I was making money in my health and wellness business, it wasn't enough to do what I needed to do. I needed to be able to cover my household bills, and have money left to invest in my business and personal development.

A regular job wasn't going to cut it. I actually attempted to get a job and it lasted all of 4 days. I needed something I could do 1-2 times per week just to make a few extra hundred every month.

I decided I would try cocktail waitressing at a nearby strip club. It had been over 8 years since I'd stopped working at the club and I'd never once considered working in that environment again until now.

I got hired on the spot and started right away. It was a hood lowkey spot not far from downtown Atlanta. It kind of reminded me of the first club I started at and I didn't know anybody in that area, so I could keep waitressing on the low.

My goal was to do it 3-4 months and invest every dollar I made into my business. I would be working 2-3 nights per week from 9pm-3am. I had to wear a black bodysuit with black fishnet stockings and flat black boots.

I made over $600 in tips my first night as a waitress and instantly felt that rush of counting cash at the end of the night again. I made money every time I went to work. A lot of the guys would suggest I dance, they claimed I would make all the money, but dancing wasn't an option. I was cool with the $300-600 a night I was making waitressing, and I couldn't wear stripper heels if I wanted to. I have a metal plate and 3 screws in my ankle, remember?

Once I started waitressing the tension at home was so thick you could cut it with a knife. Although we'd established we were breaking up, he was still pissed and concerned more than ever with what I had going on. Even my dad started noticing how much he was sweating me daily about what I had going on.

My dad told me in so many words, "Daughter, he's not it and it's best if you cut ties with him. Insecure men like him are dangerous. They will ruin everything for everybody, and you never know what they're liable to do."

He would accuse me of messing with all kinds of dudes. There was one dude in particular he swore I had something going on with, but me and the guy were just cool on social media. We'd never even met. I went to an event with a friend that was hosted by the guy, and once he found out, he made up in his mind that me and this guy were messing around.

He kept on for days accusing me of being with this dude. He'd been paying attention to every picture he liked on my Instagram page and every picture of his I liked. To me, *likes* meant nothing. *Likes* are just a part of being on social media. If I follow you and happen to see your post while I'm scrolling, I'm going to like it. It doesn't mean I like you in any real type of way.

One night he took it so far as to make up a lie saying someone he knew saw me with the dude. That was the straw that broke the camel's back for me.

At first, I just laughed, like, "Really, tell me who saw me? Call the dude right now and put him on speaker."

Of course, he wouldn't do it, but he kept pressing the issue.

Finally, he said, "I know you fuckin with that nigga, just say it."

Although me and the guy he was accusing me of had nothing going on— we'd only met once —I was so sick of his accusations. Truth be told, we were still under the same roof, but we were not together. So, when he said, "I know you fuckin with that nigga; just say it!"

I said, "YEP I am, now what???"

He lost it, started throwing things from the closet, yelling at the top of his lungs calling me every name in the book, and frantically gathering all his stuff. He always carried a gun and we had a platform bed in the master bedroom. His gun was laying on the side of the bed. He never touched the gun, but he had that same possessed look in his eye that my ex-husband had that night in the car. My dad came in to diffuse the situation, and he packed up his stuff and left.

After he left, my dad said, "See, I told you men like that are dangerous. In a situation like that, you never argue back and forth. He was out of his mind just then and there was a gun present; he could've easily shot and killed you."

He probably felt justified for the way he acted. He always found a way to rationalize his jealous insecure behavior. If I were a weak-minded woman, his attempt to flip this situation on me and every other situation he accused me of would've made me feel bad after our breakup, but I didn't.

Our relationship was officially over, and unfortunately, so was our friendship.

Even though there was a lot of unnecessary drama in our relationship and it ended on a bad note, there was still a lot of good that came from it. I'd helped him lose over 100 lbs., he'd helped me tremendously with my son, my virtual business, and I had some fun experiences with him.

After our breakup I wasn't sad at all. It was more of a relief. I felt like I'd gotten so far away from who I was in that relationship and I could now get back to me. He moved on with his life and I honestly and wholeheartedly wished the absolute best for him.

After him, I did feel like something was off with my energy and what I was putting out into the universe. Why was I attracting jealous, insecure, possessive men, why was I in this cycle of being up financially, then being down? How had I ended up back in the strip club? What was really going on with me? I needed to do some self-reflecting, so I could get to the bottom of why I was attracting certain things into my life.

I started spending more time in nature, and I decided to go on a raw food detox so I could gain better mental clarity. I started meditating more, and I did a lot of quiet introspection.

I also continued my friendship with the guy from the event. He was young, vegan, and I could have somewhat deep conversations with him that most guys his age wouldn't be ready for. So, we started hanging out more.

I was still waitressing at the club too. This club was D Boy central and it was very easy to point out the stars. All I had to do was watch how the other girls reacted to certain dudes when they walked in the club.

It felt totally different being in that environment as a waitress. There was way less pressure and it was very fast paced, and once this club got packed, it got PACKED. It had a late-night crowd so it wouldn't get super busy until 1 a.m., and between 1-3 a.m., I could make $300-600 easily.

Waitressing money at this club seemed easier than dancing money because not every dude that came in got dances, but every dude wanted something from the bar. And

167

dudes would give me outrageous tips. It was nothing for a dude to tip me a $20 or a $50 when I brought him his drink.

The money was gravy but the energy I got from some of the girls was so bad. They were BIG MAD about me being there. Again, dancers and even the bartenders and waitresses, are territorial in the club and when a new person comes in and they feel a shift in their money, the fangs come out.

It was crazy how fast I had to get back into savage mode in that environment. This time I had a set of rules, but they were a little different:

1. Don't fuck with none of these niggas.
2. Never post on social.
3. Don't trust any of the girls.
4. Get high before I go so I won't lose my mind.

I would dip off into the bathroom throughout the night to smoke and count my money so I could see where I was. Shit, I had to smoke to stay sane. The energy and vibe in the club was so bad but the money was good.

There was this one D Boy that came in one night. He was lowkey, but I knew he was one of the stars by the way the other girls reacted to him.

He called me over as soon as he got posted. When I got over to him, he was just shaking his head saying, *Mmmmmm. Mmmmmm. Mmmmmm.* He ordered a shot of Remy VSOP. When I got back, he tipped me $100. He came in often and every time he did, he broke bread with me and only me.

Sometimes he wouldn't even get a drink. He would just come post up for a bit and we would talk. Then he'd give me a couple hundred. A lot of the girls felt some type of way about it, which was something I never understood, but knew was part of the game. The customers have a right to decide who they want to spend their money on. If he used to spend money on you and now he's spending money on me, it's nothing to be mad at me about. But of course, in the club, logic is out of the window.

Me and the vegan guy from the event had hung out a few times by now and one day he said, "I have this doctor I want to take you to meet."

I said, "What kind of doctor?"

He said, "He's an herbalist and doctor of metaphysics, he's like a mind doctor."

I said, "Cool, let's go."

Little did I know, this meeting would change the trajectory of my life...

19

∞
_____ • _____

The Doctah

"When the student is ready the teacher will appear."

It was a rainy late summer day when we pulled up to his office. When we walked in, the office was very Zen and captivating. It smelled of essential oils such as tea tree, frankincense, and clove. The colors were earth tone and very peaceful, there were shelves of books and herbs, tribal decor on the walls, and beautiful plants placed around the room.

My friend shook his hand first. Then he introduced me to Doctah B. Sirius.

Doctah B walked right up to me. He was a few inches shorter than me. He didn't say a word; he just looked me dead in my eyes. It wasn't just a look though. He *pierced* me with his eyes. It was as if he looked through my whole entire soul. Then he said, "Ahhhhh I know exactly who you are!"

This little man read me like a book right there before I sat down, like he'd known me my whole life.

He knew what my hang-ups were, he knew where my insecurities were, he knew I'd been through some traumatic experiences. I thought to myself, *who the fuck is this little man and how does he know this about me?*

Doctah B asked my birthdate. When I told him, he did some quick calculations and said, "Yep, I knew it... your life path number is 1."

Then He pulled out a book called, "The Life You Were Born to Live" by Dan Milman and told me to read the section about my life path number. Prior to that day, I had no real knowledge of life path numbers, sacred geometry, parasites, or how the subconscious mind really worked.

We stayed at his office for hours and he broke information down I'd never heard before in my life. It was so deep, but it was music to my ears. I resonated with everything he was saying.

In so many words, he said, "You don't even know who you really are, you know who you think you should be."

He talked to me about subconscious programming and how the subconscious mind was like a computer and every single experience I had in my life since birth was stored there. And that just about every decision I'd made in life wasn't based off who I really was at the core. My decisions were largely based on my childhood programming.

Doctah B could also read auras, interpret energy, and read body language. It was mind blowing!

He read my aura and what he told me kind of scared me because it wasn't something I saw for myself. The Doctah told me about the light he saw around me.

He said, "You have star energy all over you, you are not a regular person, you're going to be huge, and you have a very important job to do."

Doctah B was a living legend in the world of healing and music. He talked to me about many great musicians he'd worked with in the past and he said he'd never been wrong once about someone who had the star energy around them. Doctah B wasn't the first person to express this to me. I'd had other people read my aura and tell me very similar things, but it felt more powerful coming from him.

I could've stayed and talked to him for hours, but he had other people waiting to see him. This man was a huge deal! He had clients such as Les Brown, Alice Coltraine, Michael Beckwith, and Martin Luther King III.

Before leaving, he gave me his information and told me to follow up in the coming days.

I followed up a few days later and he had instructions for me.

"This is what I want you to do first," he said as he gave me a long list of books to order. "Don't call me until you've read them all. Read them in the order I gave them to you, and I'll know if you really read them or not."

He also sent me links to videos and presentations I needed to watch. I assured him I would do it all and give him a call back when I was done.

I ordered every book on the list and went to the store to buy notebooks so I could take notes on each book. I didn't know how in the hell I was going to read all the books he gave me. I figured it was going to take forever but I also knew it was very important for my growth as a woman. I knew that if someone as wise as Doctah B advised me to read these books I needed to take action, so I got busy reading.

As I was reading and learning more about energy, vibration, the ego, and how the subconscious mind worked, I had to take a moment to check in with myself.

I'd only been waitressing at the club 2 months and I'd already gotten into two altercations with girls over customers. The first incident was minor, and the girl ended up apologizing to me, but the second incident almost led to the parking lot. That was when I said, *oh hell no, Timeout.*

I said to myself, *this is not you, you have to get high just to walk through the door and you're not even dancing. You haven't gotten into a fight since your first year in the club and you've had two altercations within weeks of each other. The energy is so low.* Look at where your mind is, you have completely backtracked, you have the fuck-niggas-get-money attitude all over you now.

You're back sliding into old spending habits and you are completely out of alignment with who you are as a woman.

By now I fully understand that money alone can't make me happy. I understand that good energy is more important than everything, and that all money isn't good money. I realized being in the club making a couple hundred dollars a night wasn't worth the bad energy that came along with me being in that environment, so I said fuck it and quit.

I did stay in contact with one person from the club and that was the lowkey D Boy, only because he'd taken an interest in my health and wellness business after mysteriously finding me on social media. Once I left the club he asked if he could take me out and I said yes. I knew he was interested in me, but I wasn't interested in being anything other than cool.

The first time I went out with him he went out of his way to show out. I was funny about people knowing where I lived, so he didn't pick me up. Instead I met him at the restaurant. He made sure I knew he drove a car that cost a quarter-of-a-million dollars when I pulled up though.

As we ate dinner, he talked about how he would spoil me if I was his, but I'd heard all of this so many times before. I could also tell he was used to controlling women with his money. He had all the tell-tale signs of an insecure possessive man who relied on money and material possessions to get women. I wasn't interested in getting romantically involved with no dude with that type of energy.

We remained cool but I knew men like him had big egos and they felt validated when they conquered certain women.

So, I got a kick out of seeing him try all his tactics on me because none of them were going to help him get what he was trying to get from me.

One day he offered to buy me a Chanel bag. I politely informed him that I wasn't interested in a Chanel bag. I'd rather invest that $5,000 into my business. To my surprise, he said okay, and because I did not want him to think I was going to fuck him, or be his girl in exchange for the money, I told him I would pay the $5,000 back as soon as I saw a return on the money. I met with him the following day and he gave me $5,000 cash in a manila envelope.

Things were going better than ever in my business. I'd invested in some higher-level coaching and learned a lot more about implementing systems that would allow me to make passive income online. I could now run my business from anywhere, so I planned a girls' trip to Vegas for my birthday. However, shortly after planning my trip my car that had been paid off for over 5 years was totaled.

I was devastated. I loved my car. I kept it in mint condition. I enjoyed not having a car note, and I was planning on giving the car to my son once he got his license. Getting a new car wasn't at all in my plan and I knew it was going to take time for me to figure out what I wanted to do. So, I decided I'd deal with the whole car situation when I got back from my Vegas trip.

Me and my girls were in Vegas for 4 days. We stayed at the Bellagio and we had a blast. We partied at Tao, Drais, and Marquee, ate at some of the best restaurants on the strip, and smoked a lot of good weed.

But before leaving Vegas something hit me though. We were still fresh into the new year and I felt as if something needed to majorly shift in my life. I suddenly felt like I'd been on a treadmill for the last few years. Yeah, I was moving but I was somehow still in the same place really.

How was I still so far from where I wanted to be, what was I doing wrong?

When I got back from Vegas, I decided on two things. The first was that I was going to take an indefinite vow of celibacy and a sabbatical from dating all together. I decided to stop talking to every dude I was connected to if I knew they wanted to be romantically involved with me. I needed a break; I'd been in relationships since I was 15 years old. I didn't want to be accountable to a man, I didn't want to get wrapped up in a man and lose focus of my goals. I didn't want to text or talk, I didn't want to go on meaningless dates for the sake of a good meal or material possessions. Shit I didn't want to be bothered, period.

The second decision I made wasn't the smartest, but I made it anyway. My car had been paid off for years before it was totaled and, in that time, I'd listened to Dave Ramsey and tried to learn more about becoming financially savvy. I knew in my heart of hearts getting a car note wasn't the best thing, but I did it anyway. I was making more money, I could afford the note, so I went and got myself a new Lexus ES. It was fully loaded. Silver with black leather interior push button start, sunroof, heated seats, reverse camera, motion sensors, and Bluetooth.

It was everything I wanted and everything I didn't need.

20

∞
_____

Mental Training Camp

"The universe is always speaking to us... sending us little messages, causing coincidences, and serendipities, reminding us to stop, look around, to believe in something else, something more." -Nancy Thayer

By now I'd completed the entire list of books Doctah B instructed me to read, and from there I started going to his office weekly for sessions.

During our first few sessions we talked about my life, my childhood, my parents, my experience as a teen mother, my relationships, and my goals.

He would interpret my body language, my tone, and the way my eyes moved when I talked about certain things. It was like he knew where I lacked confidence, he knew where the unresolved trauma was, and why it was there. He knew why I had hang-ups about men, money, and love.

He told me I leaked sexual energy that was very magnetic everywhere I went and because I wasn't 100% confident in my power as a woman, I was unconsciously attracting men who were not confident in their power as men. He said, "You're a healer by nature, your energy is therapeutic, sexy, and lively so men crave being around you, but you've been attracting patients —men who are sick and they don't have anything to give you in return energetically. So, you've been allowing them to drain you of your energy without even knowing it. This is why it's a feeling of relief when you leave them because they are no longer draining you of energy."

He asked me about my childhood, and I told him about my father going to prison, my stepfather, my siblings, how I felt about my mother, and that we always struggled but made do. He was able to point out a lot of hang ups I had about money, repressed emotions, and fear of being hurt.

He asked me to go into more detail about my mother because he could tell I had a lot of repressed anger towards her. I talked to him about why I had so much anger towards her and this was something I'd never shared in detail with anyone. My mother didn't even know I had all of this built up in me. When we got to the bottom of it, I didn't even realize how much I'd really been repressing since my childhood.

I basically told him it was her code of ethics, her rationale, and mentality that I couldn't stand. I told him I never once went to her for advice, or anything of substance because I didn't want to be anything like her. And that she really didn't even know me as a person because I'd never shared anything intimate or real about myself with her. We had a very surface level relationship. Even in adulthood, I rarely hugged, kissed, or used the words *I love you* with my mom.

I talked about her mentality about men. How she placed herself first many times, even if it was to the detriment of her own children, and how badly she talked about people. How she would gossip and spread everyone else's business, and how she'd manipulated and connived me out of money on several occasions and never apologized for it and how I never in my life felt I could trust her.

I talked about what it was like growing up with a father in prison, my feelings about my stepdad, my grandfather, other men my mom brought around us, repressed anger I had towards my son's father, and my feelings overall about men and love.

As I went into more detail about my childhood, my mother, and the men who'd been in my life, Doctah was able to point out how and why my mentality was so fucked up when it came to a lot of things. He said I had a lot of issues centered around 3 things: men, money, and love. He added that the three were all intertwined with each other and we had a lot of mud, sludge, and shit to work through.

He said, "You have an abundant mind, but you have a lot of fear-based thoughts when it comes to money, and you are unconsciously repelling money. This is why you keep going through the same cycles with money."

He asked me to describe the kind of man I desired to be with, and I went through my list of desires in a man. I even gave him a few prototypes I felt I could vibe with.

He said, "You are a very powerful woman. You don't even fully understand your power yet and it's going to take a very powerful man to balance you."

Doctah B was the realest ever when I would talk to him!

He said, "You have been dealing with men who are too weak for you. Instead of them understanding your power and wanting to balance it, they are afraid of your power, so they try to take it away from you." He predicted, "It's going to take a big, tall, strong warrior-type muthafucka who is secure in himself and on your level mentally, physically, and spiritually to come along and say let's do this."

I just laughed but I knew what he was saying was true. I told him I'd never been intentional in any of the relationships I'd been in, I'd always just wound up with men who pursued me.

He replied that he knew exactly what I desired but I was not ready for that type of man right now. I still had a lot of inner work to do.

He said, "If that man came along today you'd blow it because you're not ready for him yet, but you will be, and when you cross paths with him... when you two finally connect... that's going to be some powerful shit."

Then we got into sexual energy. I learned about sexual transmutation on a deeper level and how sexual energy is the most powerful energy on earth and we basically abuse it because we don't know how to use it to manifest our highest goals in life.

He explained why most people were emotionally unstable and a lot of it had to do with their sexual partners. I learned how energy was exchanged when a man and woman have sex and how each time a woman allowed a man to enter her he was transferring all of his energy —the good, the bad, the ugly, the trauma, the pain —and leaving that inside of her.

He explained how sacred the womb was and how a lot of women have allowed their wombs to become graveyards full of toxic negative energy from men, and how men allowed themselves to be tainted as well because each time a man enters into a toxic womb he's receiving all of that energy from every other man that has entered her as well her energy —the good, the bad, the ugly, the pain, and the trauma— so it's a cycle of dysfunctional energy being transferred between men and women who have not worked through their trauma and lack discipline when it comes to sex and their vibrational energy.

I learned a lot more about how the mind is programmed and why it's so hard for people to shift their paradigms. I'd realized this first as a health coach because I found myself coaching people on mindset more than anything else. I realized it was so hard for people to change their eating habits because they'd been programmed since birth to eat unhealthy food. I found that once a person unlearned what they'd been taught since childhood and adapted a new set of beliefs about food they would have long term success with living a healthy lifestyle.

Doctah B taught me about parasites of the mind and body and how most people unknowingly had them due to their unhealthy eating habits and unhealthy mindset. Good thing I was already a plant-based eater because I was scared straight after learning about parasites. Matter fact, I did Doctah B's elevated parasite cleanse, which is a specific detox for ridding the body of parasites, to ensure my mind and body was free from them.

I learned about the ego, also known as the conscious mind on a much deeper level and this part was very hard because I had to face a lot of my own demons.

Changing yourself is the hardest thing to do because it takes guts to look yourself in the mirror and call yourself out on your own shit. Most people want to change EVERYTHING except themselves, which is ironic because the only person on earth you can truly change is yourself.

I had to go back in hindsight and take responsibility for the role I played in a lot of unfortunate situations I'd been in. I had to forgive others, I had to look myself in the mirror, and say, "See that's where you were wrong right there."

I had to admit to being judgmental of others and of myself, I had to admit to feeling inadequate, I had to admit to my own vulnerabilities, I had to admit to being so guarded because I was terrified of being hurt, and this wasn't just a one-time thing. Part of elevating means you're constantly being a witness to your own behavior and you're constantly having to call yourself out on your own shit so you can readjust.

I had to admit to how horrible my attitude had been over the years, and to how much of a bitch I could be when I wanted to. How cold and heartless I could be. I had to admit how I had used my words to hurt and cut people very deep, how explosive my temper was, and how many situations I'd blown out of proportion. The hardest part was realizing all of this reflected what I felt on the inside at the time and a reflection of how low my energy really had been over the years.

I had to admit to the role I played in the demise of past relationships. I had to admit to knowing deep down on a certain level that none of my relationships would ever really work before even getting into them.

In hindsight, I was able to take responsibility for my part in my divorce. When things began to unravel, I blamed him for everything. I felt our marriage falling apart was his doing but after learning, growing, and maturing, I could see the role I played in our demise too. I walked down the aisle knowing we didn't have a real future together. We wanted totally different things in life. He wanted 2-3 children and wanted to live a regular life, as he put it. I knew in my core I didn't want to have children with him, and I knew I had a huge vision for my life. Playing it small and living regularly would never have cut it for me.

When you realize just about every single thing you've done in your life isn't even based on who you really are but that it's based on your childhood programming, and shit you've picked up on by default throughout life you start questioning everything. You also start connecting dots. You start seeing why you've handled certain situations in a particular way.

I'd learn to become this emotionally guarded cold hearted bitch known to have an explosive temper, who didn't really give a fuck about love or relationships, but somehow always ended up in one. I knew that wasn't really me. I really wanted to know more about who I was at the core, not the woman I'd become based on my programming, but who I really was. I got much deeper into my life path number, my personality traits, what I was inspired by, what I was attracted to most, and what felt the best to me.

Doctah B is an etymologist and he would constantly get on me about language and knowing how to use my words to affirm what I desired in life. He taught me about the real power of the words *I AM*.

He would advise me, "Stop saying *want*. You say *want* too much. To *want* something means you don't believe it's already yours."

One day I was on the way to his office for a session. I was getting off the expressway waiting for the light to turn when... *BOOM!* A raggedy ass Chevy Suburban rear ended me in my new Lexus out of nowhere. I was livid but remained calm while waiting for the police.

After getting everything squared away with the police, I proceeded to Doctah B's office. I'm fuming at this point! The whole rear of my brand-new car was smashed in and now I was late for my appointment. I kept saying to myself you have to be fucking kidding me.

When I got to Doctah B's office he could immediately tell something was wrong, so he came out to look at the car. His response?

"This is great."

I said, "Huh???"

He said, "This is great. Clearly the car needed to be hit on your way here today. It's all part of the bigger plan."

Doctah B had a great way of making me realize life was always happening for my greatest good, no matter how bad a situation looked.

By the time I left his office I didn't care one bit about the accident. The car was insured, and most importantly, I wasn't severely hurt so I saw how small of a deal it really was.

They ended up totaling my car out after the accident but this time I didn't go get another car. I got the hint. Having two cars totaled back to back had to mean something. This wasn't a coincidence.

For the next few weeks, I just kept asking the universe what it meant, and what lesson I was supposed to learn.

***

"Nothing ever goes away until it teaches us what we need to know" -Pema Chodron

I went months without a car, but I continued going to my sessions with Doctah B. I was also reading and learning on my own. Doctah would always say don't take my word on anything, always research everything on your own too, and that was something I lived by.

Doctah B had now become a real mentor. He'd taken me under his wing and selflessly dedicated hours every week to teaching me on much deeper levels about the mind, numerology, nutrition, energy, and universal laws. He was also a counselor and therapist helping me work through my trauma.

I remember him telling me once, "You know you're an anomaly, right? Most people your age aren't ready for this level of information." He added, "I know you're serious too because I've tried to scare you off a few times, but you keep coming back."

He said he knew for sure I'd say fuck it after he gave me all of those books to read, but I was hungry for the information and putting in the work to read and research wasn't going to scare me off. I was like Neo and Doctah B was like Morpheus. He'd opened my mind and eyes to a level of consciousness that was out of this world literally.

Doctah B would be on my ass too. That's the thing about having a true mentor. A real mentor is not there to coddle you, a real mentor is going to call you out on your shit.

He would call me out of the blue and say, "How are you being?" Before I could even respond he would drop some knowledge on me so deep and so on-time. Like, it would be exactly what I needed to know at that moment. It was like real telepathy.

The thing about elevating and growing spiritually is that it's all about doing the inner work, it's not about anyone or anything outside of yourself, so there's nowhere to hide and no one to blame. I would have to constantly face my own ego. The ego is where the false perceptions, self-sabotage, seeking validation, and judgement reside.

Changing yourself isn't a one-time thing. You don't wake up one day enlightened. Change occurs in different phases and stages, and it's a continual process.

I was so grateful to have someone as brilliant as Doctah B as a mentor. He would tell me about his mentor, Dick Gregory, and the 12 other mentors he had throughout his life and the lessons he learned from them.

Working with Doctah B revealed just how much trauma I'd really experienced and how events that seem to be small and meaningless can have a lasting impact on you if left unaddressed. I had so many revelations during this time.

Revelations about my parents, my relationships, and my son.

Now that I had a better understanding of mental programming I could better comprehend my own negative personality traits, I better understood my son's behavior and negative personality traits, and I could finally see why my mom moved the way she moved.

Doctah B would always say, "See you, the *real* you, she's in there and she wants to come out, but you're afraid to let her out because she is a lover. All she wants to do is be loved. She wants to give love, receive love, and spread love, but you've experienced a fair share of trauma, hurt, and pain and you have unconsciously locked the real you away."

He helped me understand why I'd locked her away. He helped me make the connection between the pain and trauma I experienced when I was 2 years old that night in 1987 when my father was taken to prison in front of me. That one event had literally affected my whole paradigm when it came to love and men, which was why I'd been so emotionally shut down and cold my entire life.

Growing up with the evil Jamaican and his explosive temper combined with my mother's manipulative narcissistic mindset, I learned to behave in a lot of undesirable ways which was a large part of why my attitude was so bad, why my temper was so explosive, and why I never had those feelings of love, empathy, or trust for my mother.

Your subconscious mind is like a recorder that has literally recorded everything that has happened in your life exactly the way it happened. Your subconscious mind never stops recording, even when you're asleep the subconscious is awake recording. Your subconscious mind has a perfect memory. It's the conscious mind, also known as the ego, that can't recall events exactly how they happened.

185

Your subconscious mind knows all your emotional triggers and its job is to make sure you respond to life based on your programming. Your subconscious has been programmed based on your parents, teachers, siblings, peers, religious faith, TV, magazines, radio, life experiences, etc. You develop your ego, the way you see yourself in the world, the way you see others in the world, and the story you tell about yourself from your programming that happens between ages of 0-7.

Doctah B explained to me that as a young child I had to lock the real me away. I had to guard her because she'd been hurt, devastated, and heartbroken when her father went to prison. And I never trusted my mother or felt she was a protector or someone I could depend on because of how she allowed the evil Jamaican to treat us and for things she did during my childhood. So, my defense was up from a very young age. He told me my energy was 95% masculine and I moved and rationalized things more like a man. He said putting your defense up about love and emotion helped you as you were growing up. You needed to have that tough layer, but now it's hindering you. You can't thrive with the same mindset and beliefs that helped you survive. He said everything is about balance. He taught me about yin and yang energy, and I discovered ways in which I could start tapping more into my feminine energy so I could be more balanced.

After each session I would reflect on our deep conversations and this helped me make so many revelations about my own life. Each time I made a new revelation it was like a layer of this shell of a woman I'd learn to become based on my programming was being peeled back and the real me was slowly being revealed.

The thing about finding yourself is that the real classroom is inside. Doctah B was providing me with the information, but it was up to me to do the real work, which was the inner work.

Doctah B would always say, "I can only provide you with the information. I can't tell you what to do or which decisions are best. Only you can decide that."

Over time I was able to see that my mom did the absolute best she could raising us based on her childhood programming and the traumatic experiences she'd been through in life. Doctah B helped me see how her unaddressed trauma and her childhood programming was transferred to us in many ways and that it wasn't really her fault because she wasn't even consciously aware of it.

When you don't address trauma it's like an illness that you can't see, taste, or touch but it's transferred and it perpetuates itself. This was very evident when I looked at the condition of my family. I was able to see that my brother was genetically predisposed to mental illness because of my parents, more so my mother, and the things he experienced during his childhood. A toxic mother is just as damaging if not more than an absent father. You never know how unresolved trauma will show up later in life or how it will affect your offspring. I now was able to see how myself and all my siblings had been affected by our childhood programming in different ways.

One thing I will say is that I never blamed my mom for my shortcomings in life ever, not once. I never felt my failures were her fault or a result of my childhood. I just took them to the chin and kept moving. Matter fact, my mother wasn't even aware of all the issues I had with her internally because I held them all in. So even though I was learning that everything that ever happened to me in my life was largely based on programming I had no control over, I still didn't feel anything that went wrong in my adult life was anyone else's fault. I took accountability for all my own bullshit.

Doctah B did help me point out a lot of positive aspects of my mother such as her allowing us to dream big and pursue anything we desired. My mom was never a dream killer. She would support any idea you had wholeheartedly, and I did love that about her. She was also very clean, organized, and cultured. She had an eye for artwork and interior design, she kept a beautiful house, and she was an avid reader, which I know played a huge role in my love for books. She graduated from GSU with two degrees despite having 7 children and that was very admirable.

She kept food on the table, and a roof over our head. She was beautiful and classy, and I had to give her props for that. Shit, raising one child was kicking my butt.

Although I still had issues with my mom's mindset, her whole code of ethics and the way she rationalized things in her mind, I was able to forgive her for a lot of stuff and release a lot of my resentment towards her. I was also able to see how many things I still needed to work on within myself as I worked through my repressed emotions for my mom. I still had a lot of judgement, bitterness, toxic energy and anger to release from my spirit.

I was able to forgive my son's father and let go of a lot of resentment I had towards him. I understood he did the best he could based on his programming and life experiences. Overall, I was grateful my son at least knew his father and had him in his life.

I also realized why it's very selfish and not a good idea at all to have children when you're young or when you have unresolved trauma present. You pass that trauma on to your kids by default and it does a huge disservice to the child and it's really unfair.

I was able to find the grace in all my past relationships. And I was grateful for each experience because each experience led me where I currently was, which was on the path of awareness, and my own self truth.

21

∞

Gut Feeling

I flew to Orlando with my son to go to my oldest sister's graduation from law school, and we had a great weekend with family and friends in celebration of my sister's success. I was very proud of her. I'd witnessed her journey and all the trials and tribulations she went through to get into law school, and there she was graduating from FAMU law, changing the narrative in our family becoming the first attorney.

A few weeks after returning from Orlando, out of the blue, I started having this sinking feeling about my business and where I was in life in general. It was so weird because things were going so well. I was finally running my business the way I'd envisioned it and making a lot of money, but I wasn't happy or fulfilled with it. I felt as if it was no longer for me, like I'd outgrown it, or like something was missing, but I couldn't quite put my finger on it.

By now I'd worked with a few different business coaches and I'd really taken a liking to the more technical side of digital business. I was more interested in how automated systems such as marketing funnels worked and that was what I spent most of my time learning more about when I wasn't working with Doctah B. I no longer had the same level of passion for being a health coach as I did when I first started. Honestly, I grew tired of trying to convince people to care about their own lives. I hadn't mentioned what I was feeling about my business to anyone.

One day, Doctah B called and said, "Listen, the way you're going about doing this health coaching thing isn't really you."

I said, "What do you mean? That's my purpose, it's what I'm supposed to be doing."

He said, "Well I listen to you, I pay attention to your tone, and your eyes when you talk about certain things. This digital, techie stuff... that's you, that's what you may want to consider doing," he concluded. "You light up when you start talking that techie shit. The average person wouldn't want to be bothered with that stuff, but you are so passionate when you speak about it. A regular person couldn't stay in a room behind a computer screen for hours learning this shit."

I knew he wasn't wrong because I'd previously thought about switching over and doing business consulting online, but I'd been doing health coaching for a while. Health coaching was what I was known for and I'd been through so many ups and downs trying to grow the business so I couldn't just walk away from it. Or could I?

Doctah B said, "I'm not gonna tell you what to do, it's just something to think about."

I took a few months to think about it and I decided I was ready to step away from health coaching so I could focus on going in a new direction. I realized I wanted to use my other gifts, such as my analytical mind, online expertise and background in business economics so I could help people in a different type of way.

So, I found a new business coach to work with but not just any coach. He came highly recommended and was a multi-millionaire himself, so I was excited. None of my other coaches prior to him had been millionaires. It was going to cost me thousands of dollars to work with him though like more money than I'd ever invested into my personal development. In fact, it was damn near going to break the bank but I felt I needed to roll the dice and bet on myself if I really wanted to shift directions and take my new business to the next level.

My mindset at the time was like this: I have a new millionaire coach and because I'm helping people with business now instead of health, I can charge more money for my services because I knew from experience that unfortunately people valued making more money over getting healthy. From the results I'd seen other people who worked with this coach get, I just knew I'd be making 7 figures in no time.

So, I put all my eggs in one basket. I'd gone months without a car. I had money saved and I knew I was about to start making more money, so I went and got a new Lexus GS350. It was fully loaded with a sunroof. It was black, with black interior, and presidential tint on the windows. It felt like I was driving a spaceship and I loved that the tint was so dark no one knew it was me. I wanted a change of scenery too, so I decided to move to a new 2-story loft.

My dad had been living with me for a year and a half and I'd enjoyed having him there. I'd really gotten to know him on more than a surface materialism level. This time around I got the loving nurturing father. I'd gotten to see how intellectually brilliant he was, how knowledgeable he was, and how abundant his mind was. My dad taught me a lot about knowledge of self, spirituality, business, and he was an excellent cook. We would stay up for hours talking, he had the best stories literally his life stories were better than watching a movie. I'd be busy working on my computer all day in my room and he'd come knock on my door with the best home cooked meals. His soups were my favorite, especially the coconut curry vegetable soup.

I found that I was a lot more like my dad than I was my mom and we had more of an organic chemistry with each other.

My lease was almost up, and I decided it would be best if my dad went to stay with my brother so me and my son could have some time together, just us two. Me and my son had been through a lot of changes since my divorce. We'd moved around a lot and I just felt we were not as connected as we'd been before. He would be graduating from high school soon and on his way out into the world and I wanted some quality time to spend with him.

Once I made the decision to move, something in my spirit told me to get rid of everything before leaving and to only take the bare minimum with me to my new place. It was like I wanted to get rid of everything that'd been associated with my ex or any other man, and any other low vibrational experience. I wanted my new place to have brand new energy, I didn't want to bring any luggage from the past. So, I had an estate sale. I got rid of all the furniture, appliances, and I'd built back up a pretty nice wardrobe and I got rid of most of that too. Once the estate sale was over me and my son prepared to move to our new place.

Right before moving there was one more thing I needed to do. I just felt I needed to take a break from the outside world. The internal urge to do this was so strong and it came out of the blue. My gut feeling told me I needed to silence all the outside noise and really get off the grid so I could focus on my elevation and listen to my own inner voice. I decided to take an indefinite break from social media, and I decided I didn't want to communicate with anyone outside of my mentor, business coach, and two other people.

I sent a mass text message to my family and close friends letting them know I was off the grid and unavailable to talk, go out, or have company unless it was an emergency. I told them not to worry, I wasn't losing my mind. I just wanted time to myself and that I'd reach out if I needed anything. I explained I didn't know how long this phase was going to last but I'd let them know when I was out of it. I asked them to respect my wishes. I don't know where this all came from, but I knew it wasn't something I had to do.

***

"A caterpillar must endure a season of isolation before it turns into a butterfly. Embrace the time you have alone it will only make you stronger" -Steven Aitchison

Things were great when I first moved to my new place. My loft was very contemporary, with two stories. The master was on the second floor. I had a huge jacuzzi tub in my bathroom, and a huge walk in closet. My son's room was downstairs, and we could see the Atlanta skyline from our balcony. I would sit on the balcony with a joint every night looking at the moon and stars sometimes for hours. I was at complete peace. It was exactly what I needed.

I got rid of my TV before moving so I didn't watch TV at all. I spent most of my day reading, researching, and implementing what I was learning from my new business coach.

By this time, Doctah B was teaching me a lot more about epigenetics, how trauma is genetically passed down, visualization, neural pathways, and reprogramming the subconscious mind. I was introduced to Neville Goddard, Dr. Bruce Lipton, and Reverend Ike. I was given more books to read, more lectures to watch and I began listening to meditative music tuned to vibrational frequencies that promote healing such as 528hz and 432hz each night as I drifted off to sleep and each morning before starting my day.

Everything in the universe, including you, is vibrating at a certain frequency. Because you and everything around you *is* energy. The energy of the Earth vibrates at a 528Hz frequency which is the same frequency as the universal healer of all things: Love.

The frequency of 432Hz is powerful. It can help repair and restore DNA, bring love, peace, harmony and joy to everything around it.

I became very clear on my higher goals and what I desired to manifest in my life. I was so excited about what I was working toward and I thought I was ready for the next level, but life has a way of showing you different.

I didn't realize I was still hindering myself from elevating until I got to know some of the other people in the coaching group. I thought the next level meant driving a luxury car and living in a two-story loft, but I couldn't have been more wrong.

Some of the people in my group were making six figures per month and they were just getting to the point of driving luxury cars and living in expensive homes. Others were driving regular cars, and some were even rooming with friends. They were keeping their overhead low so they could focus on getting to the next level for real.

Instead of buying luxuries they were focused on staying down, keeping expenses low, while they scaled their businesses to the 7-figure level. They were not wearing designer labels, nor were they interested in flexing for the 'Gram. They were lowkey, a lot of them didn't even have social profiles.

They were also very open to sharing information. They wanted to give you as much game as possible on how to succeed in business and life. I learned about taxes, life insurance policies, and how people with money really move and maintain their wealth.

I was very grateful to be surrounded by wealthy people willing to share the game, but I also realized I was not wealth minded at all. I had a poverty-based mindset. For one I was financially illiterate. It's very hard to become wealthy if you don't understand how money works.

For example, understanding the difference between assets and liabilities is financial literacy. An *Asset* is something that pays you, while a *Liability* is something you pay for. So, realizing my brand-new Lexus and loft were both liabilities was a hard pill to swallow. What was even harder was realizing how much money I'd blown in my life on liabilities, such as designer clothes, bags, and shoes.

I started breaking down even my most mundane expenses. For instance, I calculated how much money I'd spent over the years getting my nails done and it was over $50,000. I was flabbergasted by that number. How the fuck had I spent over 50 racks on nails, yet I didn't own one single asset???

All of this confirmed I still had a poverty-based mindset. People with a wealthy mindset know you buy luxuries last, after the assets have started paying dividends. Here I was living in a luxury condo and driving a luxury car with no assets, therefore no dividends.

The conversations wealth-minded people have versus the conversations poverty-minded people have are totally different.

Poverty-minded people gossip and talk about spending money. Wealth-minded people talk about innovative ideas and earning and investing money. Wealth-minded people talk about buying low and selling high. Poverty-minded people brag about paying full price. I learned wealth is very quiet and it's very discreet. Whereas poverty is very loud and ostentatious.

The more I realized my mind was still in poverty the more I realized why I was still so far from reaching my financial goals. How could I be asking the universe for wealth and abundance and I wasn't even prepared for it.

The thing about the universe is it responds to your energy, not your words, but the emotions and feelings behind your thoughts. So, in my conscious mind, also known as the ego mind, I was thinking I was somehow exempt and that I would be able to keep my car and condo and still get to the next level. But energetically, I was saying something totally different. With my energy I was telling the universe I was ready to learn what I needed to learn so I could elevate and get to the next level in my life.

"When things fall apart, consider the possibility that life knocked it down on purpose. Not to bully you, or to punish you, but to prompt you to build something that better suits your personality and your purpose. Sometimes things fall apart so better things can fall together." -Unknown

In a domino effect manner, all hell broke loose. Literally one thing went wrong, and everything collapsed after. The first thing was realizing, although I'd invested a large amount of money to work with my coach, I still needed a lot more capital to see a return on my investment and I didn't have access to more capital.

I was spread extremely thin, financially, because my monthly overhead was so high. My income was very inconsistent now that I was shifting the focus of my business and my bills were piling up at lightning speed.

I was never one to ask for help from my family. My dad was in prison 20 years of my life and other than my mom helping me after my divorce, I never went to her for help with any of my problems. She remarked to me once when I was in my early 20's that I was only one of her seven children that she never had to worry about. She said for some reason she just always knew I was going to be okay. So, I made it my business not to go to my mom when I had a problem.

I had more money going out than coming in. I didn't want to admit it, but I was living way above my means. There's a huge difference between being able to pay for something and being able to afford something. I was barely getting by with my bills. I even started back using credit cards, something I'd stayed away from since I was 19 years old, just so I could make ends meet. I was in over my head. It was clear I couldn't afford the lifestyle I was living.

Me and my son were right back where we were after my divorce. But it was even worse because he was in high school, a prominent high school at that. He had friends living in multimillion-dollar homes, and a lot of celebrity children went to his school. So, the pressure to dress a certain way was on.

He no longer wanted Jordans, he wanted Off-White, Margiela, and Yeezy's. I would tell him how ridiculous it was to expect high-end fashion in high school. I told him how even my dad, with all the money he had when I was in high school, still wouldn't buy me Gucci and Prada. He would tell me I had to stay in my lane. But my son didn't understand my perspective. He wanted what he saw at school and on social media.

I knew I had to do something quick when I looked up and had 4 accounts in the negative and a $900 cell phone bill looming over my head. Out of utter desperation, I decided to give Uber a chance, but it wasn't worth it. I was driving a car that required premium gas so just about everything I made went to gas, and after having a drunk passenger get in one Saturday night, after only a few weeks I decided it wasn't for me.

We barely had food in the house. I know I could've gone and applied for food stamps or gotten a 9-5 but I didn't want to. I wanted to figure this out on my own. Although I swore to myself when I had my son that I'd never get on welfare, there were a few times I'd gotten food stamps, like after my divorce, for example. I always felt some type of way about using them. I don't know why but using food stamps made me feel inadequate. So, although I was headed straight for *Brokeville* and everything around me was falling apart, I refused to go apply for food stamps or get a job.

There were several dudes I could've called and asked for money, but I refused. I was in full monk mode; I didn't want to call and ask anyone for money.

I called Doctah B one day to ask him for advice. I told him everything that was going on with me financially, with my business, my son, everything. He sat on the other end of the phone silently then he finally instructed that I must surrender to it.

I thought to myself, *Is that it? Where's the wisdom, where's the spiritually deep advice?* I wanted him to tell me something I could magically do to stop everything from falling apart. But that was it? "Surrender to it".

I was kind of angry at him and I thought he was crazy. What did he mean surrender? I'm a Capricorn, my life path number is 1, I'm a fighter, I don't have surrender in my

DNA! What type of advice is that? Those were the thoughts going through my head.

He said, "There must be one person you can call to help with your living situation. Think of one person you can trust that will respect your privacy and understand what you are going through."

After speaking with Doctah B I took a few days to think. I knew I couldn't call my mom. She would spread my business and slander my name faster than a wildfire spreading in the forest. And my siblings were busy living their own lives, in no position to help me. I could only think of one of my cousins that I would be willing to call and ask for help.

He was a photographer and we'd worked together several times. He did all my photography and videography when I was a hairstylist and a health coach. I knew he lived alone, traveled a lot, he was very kind, and always willing to go above and beyond for others. Still I was very hesitant to call and ask him if me and my son could crash at his place while I fell apart and figured my life out.

But I was at my wits end. I was broke, my cell phone was about to get cut off, and my credit cards were maxed out. So, although I was apprehensive, I made the call. I explained the entire situation to my cousin and told him I would pay him back for everything once I got on my feet.

Before I could finish explaining he said, "Sure, y'all can come on up. You can have the upstairs and I'll make some room for your stuff in the garage," he decided. "And you're family, you don't owe me anything. I'm more than happy to help."

I told him where I was in terms of being in solitude. I told him I didn't want anyone to know I was staying with him and he agreed to respect my privacy.

My cousin lived in a nice area in Cobb County about 30 minutes from downtown Atlanta. Between giving stuff away and getting rid of stuff, I didn't have much to take. So, I packed the remainder of our stuff in black trash bags and made the move to my cousin's.

School was out when I made the move, so my son was at his dad's for the first few weeks, and I was at my cousin's by myself for the most part. When my cousin wasn't out of town, he stayed gone all day, which was cool. I had a lot of quiet time alone.

Those first few weeks were extremely hard. I felt lost, I felt like a complete failure. I didn't have an appetite, I had so much anxiety I couldn't sleep at night, and I was blaming myself for everything. I was questioning all the inner work and spiritual work I'd been doing. This wasn't what I desired to manifest in my life, why was this happening to me?

I felt alone, like there was no guidance from the creator, from the universe, my inner voice, or Doctah B. I couldn't see or hear anything. Everything was dark and foggy. It felt as if I was in the middle of the ocean on a raft with no land in sight and no idea which way to go.

I remember waking up one morning sitting in the middle of the air mattress I was sleeping on, looking around the room at all of our shit in trash bags thinking, "This can't really be my life right now. Shit was all good just a year ago." All these emotions started rushing through me and then the air mattress collapsed. I could hear the air seeping out and as it deflated, I just sat there and laughed to keep from crying.

For the next few weeks, I gave in to doing absolutely nothing other than eating when I could stomach it. I would literally wake up crying every morning. I couldn't meditate, I couldn't read anything, I didn't even want to open the blinds. All I did was lay in the dark, smoke weed, cry, and listen to oldies, mostly Stevie Wonder.

After going through some of the darkest moments of my life, feeling like the biggest failure, and worst mother on the planet, Doctah B called. He said he had a book that he thought would really help me right now.

"I'll send you the audio version," he said. He also assured me that I was prepared to continue going through this dark night of the soul and that I'd be grateful for it all in due time.

The dark night of the soul can be described as a period of spiritual bleakness, disconnection, and emptiness in which one feels lost and totally separated from the Divine. It is a journey of awakening and tapping into your true self.

I wasn't really into audiobooks, but I didn't have a dime to my name to order the paperback so when he sent the audio version, I immediately began listening. The book was called, *How to Prosper in Hard Times*. I finished the audio book within days and from there I was compelled to re-read some of the other books that greatly helped me in the past. I re-read, *Ask and it is Given, The 4 Agreements, The Alchemist*, and a few others.

After a few weeks passed I started feeling a little better in my spirit. I was no longer waking up in tears, I was able to start back doing my morning meditation, working out, saying my affirmations, and I started keeping a gratitude journal. I was also spending copious amounts of time in nature.

My cousin had a beautiful backyard. I would sit out there barefoot so I could ground. Grounding is connecting your bare feet to the earth so you can absorb the therapeutic electrical charges.

Grounding improves your sleep, reduces stress, reduces pain, and inflammation in the body. So, I'd sit out with my herbal tea and a book for 2-3 hours at a time. I would breathe in the fresh air, move my arms with the wind, and listen to the music of the birds, squirrels, and chipmunks running through the woods.

Although I was feeling better, I still had a lot of stress and anxiety over the deep financial hole I dug myself into. My cell service was disconnected, my car note was delinquent, I had 4 negative accounts, I was sleeping on an air mattress, and my business was barely hanging on by a thread.

Feeling stuck is an understatement. I was paralyzed. I didn't know which way to move, how was I going to get out of the mess I'd made. I couldn't even think straight. Every time I thought about how deep the hole was, I got overwhelmed and frustrated.

I tried my best to rationalize keeping my Lexus, but I knew I never wanted to be in this place again and this was a lesson I freaking missed when I totaled the other cars. I couldn't afford to have to learn this again, so I was ready to set myself free from the albatross the Lexus had become. But letting the car go was easier said than done. I'd had my own car since 18 and I was mortified at the thought of having to ask my cousin for rides on top of me already staying at his place.

After my mind was made up about letting the car go, it became a waiting game. My plan was to drive the car until they found it. I drove the car for about 3 months and then one night my son called for me to pick him up for work. I walked out into the driveway and the Lexus was gone.

My cousin and I picked my son that night and when he got home, I explained what happened with the car. I could see it in my son's eyes that he was so disappointed in me. Not only was I broke, not only were we living with someone else yet again, but I didn't have a car to get us to and fro. This was a new low.

Although I knew letting the car go was best, I still felt terrible afterwards.

Part 4: The Monarch Butterfly Emerges

22

∞
_____

Failure is the Best Teacher

"Just when the caterpillar thought the world was over,
it became a butterfly" -Unknown-

This was it. I was officially at my rock bottom. All my greatest fears were realized, I'd taken so many losses back to back I felt there was nothing else to lose. All I could do now was completely surrender to what I was going through, and so I finally did.

I gave myself permission to let go of the stress, anxiety, fear, and shame. I literally busted up laughing at myself like, *Damn, you really fucked shit up, huh?* From there, I was able to accept where I was at and I knew it was only temporary.

There's a peace, liberation, and calmness that comes along with being at rock bottom. You no longer have to pretend, you no longer have to stress about holding it all together because you've lost it all, you're down so low you have to find grace in knowing the only place you can go from there is up.

At this time, I'd been celibate and on my sabbatical from dating for over a year. I changed my number and only gave it to a select few people. I was off social media unless it had to be for business. I didn't have a car or any money so there was no eating out, going out, no nothing. It was just me and my thoughts.

I felt bare, naked, and completely vulnerable but I had no choice other than to continue going through this dark night of the soul.

At first all I could think about was losing my car and how I wound up in my financial mess in the first place. It's easy to point fingers and blame others but I had to do the mature thing, which is always the hardest thing. I had to take accountability and I had to understand where I went wrong if I truly wanted to learn the lesson I was meant to learn.

The more I thought about it the clearer it became. I was still seeking validation. I was still buying into the big picture of the masses and I was still relying on things outside of myself for happiness.

Why did I feel I needed to drive a luxury car or live in an expensive condo to feel important and successful? Who was I trying to get approval from? Whose standards was I trying to meet, who was I trying to keep up with and why?

As I was going through this extremely dark time, I began asking the creator, calling on the ancestors, and speaking to the Universe asking for clarity, and understanding. Nothing happened immediately, but over time it all started making sense.

I started to see my life as this huge puzzle with pieces scattered all over the place because I wasn't in alignment with who I really was. The pieces were now coming together and I was seeing life from a totally different perspective.

I lived my entire life based off of programming I had no control over and although I'd done a lot of hard work unlearning paradigms, thoughts, and beliefs that were not serving me or my higher purpose, I was still allowing my programming to control me in a lot of undesirable ways.

Once I realized how mentally controlled I was by material possessions my entire paradigm shifted. I'd been programmed since childhood to feel I needed name brand clothes, expensive shoes, and other things outside of myself to feel happy, adequate, and important in the world.

And because of that I lived in a mental prison of validation seeking. I started to see that I needed to hit rock bottom and I had to get into the financial mess I was in so I could learn some valuable lessons, not just money but about life too.

It was as if I removed myself from the big picture of the masses and I was now looking at the bigger picture from outside of the frame. I realized how much of a puppet I'd been trying to live up to standards that were created to make people feel inferior to begin with.

I thought of how silly I'd been trying to keep up with the Joneses when the Joneses are nothing but a façade. I thought about how much money I wasted over the years buying stuff to look like I had my shit together. I promised myself: never again. I will never be controlled by anything outside of myself, I will never place value on myself or another being based on material possessions, I am confident and secure in myself regardless of what's going on outside of me.

Don't get me wrong, I don't feel like there's anything wrong with driving luxury cars, wearing designer clothes, flying private, or any of that if you can afford it and if you are not placing your self-worth in those things.

I *do* believe there's something wrong with feeling like you NEED those things to be happy, to feel important, or to feel confident in who you are. If you want nicer things that you really can't afford just so you can show them off on social media, boost your ego, or to make others feel inferior, it's time to do some soul searching.

As more time went on and as I tuned deeper into my own mind and spirit, I was no longer mad or asking why about my situation. Instead I was extremely grateful for it. I was grateful I lost the car, lost the condo, and ruined my credit, because I was freeing myself from the very thinking that got me into that situation to begin with.

Because we are taught subconsciously from childhood to search outside of ourselves for everything, we spend our lives looking for love, happiness, success, self-worth, and God in all of the wrong places, and we find short lived false happiness in material stuff that doesn't really mean much when you get down to the core of it.

I thought about my life and realized I'd already been the "successful" person. Since success in our society is based on material possessions, marital status, and college degrees.

I was a college graduate, married to a tall, handsome guy who drove a luxury car, I was a world traveler, eating at five-star restaurants, and going on lavish shopping sprees. Yet none of that stuff fulfilled me on a soul level so I was constantly seeking outward for more stuff... more bags, more shoes, more titles, more accolades to make me happy.

That was the mistake I'd been making my whole life. Happiness is an inside job; you must find happiness inside of yourself first before anything outside of you can truly be fulfilling. Happiness does not come to you; it comes from inside of you. Life isn't about finding something or someone to make you happy and complete, it's about knowing you are whole and complete and being happy just as you are.

As I could see the puzzle pieces of my life coming together, I felt more confident, more free, more beautiful, sexier, happier, and more powerful than ever before.

From the outside looking in, one might have thought I was crazy. I didn't have a car, any money, or a pot to piss in. How could I possibly feel good about myself when everything in my world was a mess? But it was all about what I was feeling inside, and internally, I felt marvelous. I could feel a major shift happening. I could feel the small me, the old programmed version of me, slowly disappearing and I could feel this new, powerful, confident woman with new energy, and a new paradigm emerging, and it was a beautiful feeling.

I realized I didn't need validation from anyone because I was a God in complete control of my life and everything I needed was already within. I was enough just as I was and all I needed was to be in control of my own mind, my own thoughts, my own energy, and my own vibration to manifest exactly what I desired in life when it came to health, wealth, love, and relationships.

I thought more about my past relationships and my experiences with men in general, and up until this point I'd never given any real focus to what I desired in a fulfilling relationship. My focus was always on two major things: my son and making money. A relationship was never really a priority to me.

I didn't even know what a healthy relationship was. I'd never seen an example of one. Growing up all the women in my family were in toxic, unhealthy relationships with men they settled for. My mom, aunts, and grandmother all had the same attitude about men. *Men get on my damn nerves, they're all full of shit, I don't want to live with one or marry another one.* That was the gist of their feelings about men. There was never any positive talk or conversations about men, love, or healthy relationships.

So, my attitude was similar and even though I always wound up in relationships I always cared more about pursuing my goals than I did a relationship.

I was cleaning up listening to Stevie Wonder one night when Love's, "In Need of Love Today" came on and

210

although I'd listened to that song several times before, this night I HEARD it for the first time. I felt every word to my core, as if he was singing the song to me about me. I started thinking back to my beginning sessions with Doctah B and him saying the real me was a lover, but I was afraid to let her out. The deeper I thought about it, the clearer this huge revelation I was about to make became.

How can you really love yourself when you don't know yourself, how can you really love yourself if you're afraid to be yourself? How can you truly love another unconditionally, when you don't love yourself unconditionally?

Love was all I could think about and I had a burning desire to understand it on a deeper level. I created this vortex of love around me. I stopped listening to rap and hip-hop altogether. My ears only wanted to listen to love music. We invite a lot of negativity into our lives by default without realizing it through what we listen to, watch, read, and who we follow on social media. I had to really detox from everything negative so I could get aligned with my highest vibration. So, I would listen to The O' Jay's, The Isley Brothers, Patti Labelle, Sade, H.E.R., Daniel Caesar, Jhene Aiko and Stevie Wonder all day. Even when I worked out, I was listening to love music.

I read love quotes, I wrote about love, and if I was watching something, it was about love.

I began thinking deeply about relationships and the kind of relationships I desired to have with everyone; my son, my siblings, my parents, business associates, and for the first time ever, I got intentional about the kind of relationship I desired to be in romantically. I mean the real stuff, not just the physical attributes I desired a man to have, but the kind of energy I desired to feel and the kind of woman I desired to be in a relationship too.

I talked with my mentor for hours one day about love, my beliefs about love, my hang-ups about love, and I was able to connect a lot of dots. After reading a book called, "The Mastery of Love", I made the toughest revelation of them all: I'd NEVER really been in love with a man before.

I didn't really know how to love a man because I was so guarded and afraid to feel and very unclear on who I was. So, in my past relationships, strong feelings were present at the time, but it wasn't real love. It wasn't deep or unconditional, it was very surface level, conditional, and toxic it was a very small incomplete version of my love because that was all I knew how to give.

I thought back to the times when I prided myself on not having feelings and not giving a fuck, when I thought being cold hearted was okay, when I thought showing emotions was weak. That's a really sad way to live life. Our very nature as human beings is to feel and to love but when you've experienced pain, hurt, and trauma it hardens you, it numbs you, and you learn to avoid feeling at all costs. That hardness does something to you internally, it's like a slow poison.

Reading about love, listening to love music, and loving myself better made me think about the kind of love I desired to be in. I sat quietly and thought about how nice it would be to really love the fuck out of a man unconditionally in this lifetime.

Not just any man, though. I desire for him to be an alpha male, purpose driven, and superior in his masculinity, unshakably confident and secure in who he is on this earth. A man with an abundant mindset, a true friend and companion, a strong man who understands what having a strong woman means, a man brave enough to do the inner work, a man to elevate mentally, physically, and financially with, a man to be completely vulnerable and real with, a man to have a love rooted in freedom and trust with.

I also thought about the kind of love I desired to give him, the kind of woman I could now be in a relationship, and how fortunate we'd both be to experience this kind of love. I was looking forward to him experiencing this version of me being the first to receive my real unconditional love, being nurturing, supportive, keeping him on his toes, helping him elevate mentally, physically, spiritually, and financially, being his peace, raising his vibration, being silly, having fun, and next realm experiences in the bedroom.

And no I wasn't going to actively seek him out, I wasn't going to get on dating sites, or go to happy hour searching for him, I was simply going to focus on being the energy I desired to attract and that was it.

The flower doesn't chase the butterfly, the flower blooms and the butterfly is attracted to its sweet smell. I felt the same way about attracting the type of man I truly desired.

Although being celibate for over a year was one of the hardest things I'd ever done, I found an ironic joy in the level of discipline I was attaining from it. Mastering what I put in my body, and mastering my sexual energy was extremely powerful. This was me loving myself in a real way, not just saying the words to myself but taking actions that proved I was making my health and well-being a priority. My energy and vibration being in the right place was more important to me than anything.

But I'm human and I happen to be a woman with a very high libido, so yes, of course I had urges and often felt horny out of my mind. So, I learned how to harness that energy. Sometimes I harnessed it into physical activities like working out. Other times, I allowed myself to feel it. I would use my imagination to visualize how bomb my next sexual

213

experience would be, the kind of energy that would be present in the room, and I had a particular man in mind, so visualizing was fun!

I didn't have a time limit on remaining celibate, I wasn't waiting for marriage or anything like that it was more of a mind over matter thing. It was going to take more than good looks and financial success for me to have a sexual exchange. A man would have to be on a certain vibrational frequency for me to even feel sexually attracted to him. I'd learned too much and done way too much inner work; my womb was too sacred to be willing to have a quick thrill with a dude whose energy would taint me. So, I was willing to be patient.

In the meantime, my goal was to focus on loving myself and others more.

Love is the universal healer, love is the highest vibration one can exist in, love is the key to good health, wealth, abundance and prosperity. Once I embraced the vibration of love, I began feeling like the Phoenix slowly rising from the ashes, the revelations were coming back to back and they were crystal clear.

Love was the thing this whole journey of self-awareness and self-truth started with. I made a decision after breaking my ankle to love myself better by adapting a healthy lifestyle which led to a series of what seemed to be unfortunate events, but in reality, all of those unfortunate events led me here exactly where I needed to be. Bare, stripped of all my "cool", vulnerable, and cash poor. Because I was becoming soul rich I could finally do the hardest part of my inner work, and that was to become the real me, the lover, the alchemist acting solely for the highest good of all, transforming everything into love.

This would be no easy task, love, feeling deeply, empathy and expressing emotions were all things that felt very unnatural to me. Before now, I never wanted to feel too much, nurturing didn't come naturally, I wasn't the one to call for comfort when a family member or friend felt sad and needed empathy. I was the one to call when you needed motivation or a laugh.

Even with my own son, now that he was older, connecting emotionally didn't always come easy. My son knew I loved him, I told him every single day. I gave him a hug and kiss every day when I dropped him at school, he never went without, there was always dinner on the table, but there was still an emotional disconnect. I was always very hard and aggressive with him. There wasn't a lot of nurturing, my patience with my son always ran thin, he saw the explosive side of my temper more than anyone else, and with money being tight as of late, I'd become annoyed by his most basic requests.

My son would be graduating from high school soon and I felt I hadn't taught him enough, instilled enough, nurtured enough, or given enough guidance. My son was a direct reflection of who I was in a lot of ways before I became aware, which was expected because I was lost, unaware, hotheaded and misguided during the years where most of his childhood programming took place.

That was a wakeup call for me. He was my son, I raised him, and no I wasn't going to take responsibility for all his mistakes and mishaps, but I knew I couldn't pretend to be exempt either.

How many times had he heard or seen me explode on people over the years, how many inappropriate conversations did he hear? How many times did he see me and his father fight when he was a baby, what had he picked up on in the backseat listening to all of the trap music I played in the car when he was a young kid? What about the

215

movies I let him watch, how had my lack of patience and explosive temper affected him?

We like to think kids are too young to remember things. Yeah, in their conscious mind they may not remember the details, but their subconscious mind remembers it ALL perfectly and they react in life based on their subconscious programming.

I wasn't beating myself up as a mother. I was just being honest with myself. I also thought about the great experiences my son had like traveling to The Bahamas, Africa, and Mexico all before age 10 and how seeing the world opened his mind at a young age. My son was a very abundant thinker, and my son knew he had greatness within himself.

I thought about reading with him every night when he was in elementary and how his teachers would comment that they could tell I read with him at home because he reads exceptionally well in class. I thought about the life I'd given my son in the context of me being a teen mom.

According to the big picture of the masses, I was supposed to be a dropout, with five kids, 3 baby daddies', on Section 8, doing custodial work. And I didn't fall under any of those statistics. I'd done the absolute best I knew how to do up until this point and I was proud overall, but I knew there was room for a lot of improvement.

So, the first relationship I felt I needed to direct my love to was my relationship with my son.

23

∞

My Sun

Our relationship was far from the traditional mother and son relationship. I had him when I was 17. By the time he was in high school our relationship was more like a big sister little brother relationship. A lot of people spoke negatively about my son, predicted he'd be just like his dad or worse, but I didn't give a fuck I loved my son unconditionally and I couldn't solely fault him for a lot of his actions because at the core I knew a lot of his issues stemmed from him being raised by two kids, who came from dysfunction and trauma. So the one person I could always find empathy for was my son because I brought him into this world he was the only person on earth I felt I actually owed something to and would be willing to die for and ride for no matter what.

I gave my son space to be himself too, I allowed him to think for himself, and I allowed my son to have an opinion, we talked to each other in a tone that was atypical for mother and son we talked to each other very straightforward like friends, a lot of people on the outside looking in did not understand our dynamic but it was what it was for us.

The first thing I wanted to do was check in with him, I wanted to know what his life was like, I wanted to know what he was feeling, I wanted to know what it was like being a young black man in our current society. When I was unaware, caught up, "living my best life", I never thought about his world being different as a young black man than mine, now that I was aware I wanted to connect with him better and this was something I needed to understand in order to do that.

One night me and my son talked for hours and he really painted the picture for me. He told me ever since the age of about 13 he could feel and see he was black. I asked what he meant and he said you know the way white people look at me when I walk in a store... my son wore his hair in dreads and he said ma when you look like me with hair like this it makes white people feel some type of way, he said when the cops pass me and my friends it's like they're passing us in slow motion they want to find the smallest reason to say something, he said being young and black you just know you have a target on your back.

Having that conversation with him was such an eye opener, because it made me realize how many assumptions I'd made about his life and how I couldn't relate to nor did I understand what he was going through emotionally as a young black man.

I had no clue he felt this way and how could I? I'd never asked him. Because I'd never in my life experienced feeling direct discrimination because I was black, I assumed the same for my son. I didn't know what it was like to feel what he described as knowing you have a target on your back because you are black.

I wanted my son to take pride in who he was I never wanted him to feel like he had to conform to make anyone else feel comfortable, I wanted him to know the brilliance of black people, and I wanted him to understand he may never change the way others view him but he could change the way he viewed himself.

So, the first thing I did was talk to him about history. I wanted my son to know real black history, I wanted to him to really understand that our history as a people didn't start with slavery and that black people were the original people on this earth, and I wanted him to know about black wall street, and all of the inventions and patents black people were responsible for so we had conversations and watched a lot of documentaries together: *Hidden Colors, 1804* about the Haitian Revolution, we watched *Guns, Germs, and Steel*, we talked about *Marcus Garvey, Malcom X, The Black Panther Party, The Nation of Islam, the Nubians*, and about Mansa Musa the richest man who ever lived.

I talked to my son about the mind and everything I'd learned about the subconscious and programming I gave him books to read and YouTube videos to watch. I know a lot of what we talked about went in one ear and out of the other but more than anything I wanted to plant seeds of knowledge. I wanted my son to understand he was in complete control of his own destiny in life. I wanted him to understand the God within himself, and I wanted him to understand how powerful his thoughts were and that there was only a target on his back if he believed there to be one.

I talked to him about how his thoughts created his reality, I told him about a conversation me and his grandpa had when he came home from prison. I told my dad I'd accepted the fact that he'd die in prison and he told me he knew in his mind he would not die there he knew he would be free again and that he used his mind to see his way out of a 50-year death sentence. I told my son all he needed in life was to understand how to control his own mind, his own thoughts, and emotions and he could, be, do and have anything he desired.

I told my son yes I know racism, sexism, discrimination, ignorance, and injustice exists but I also know you have the power within to be do and have whatever you put your mind to in spite of all of that because you are the architect of your own life, you decide who you desire to be and what you deserve to have in this lifetime no one else.

I said to him there are a lot of fucked up things happening in the world, but I don't choose to focus my energy on the problems, I focus all my energy on the solutions. I said if everyone were the best versions of themselves most problems would no longer be. I told him the only thing I knew I could change on this earth for sure was myself so that's why I put so much emphasis on eating healthy, working out 5 days a week, spending time in nature, reading, getting proper rest, and investing in my personal development, because I was focused on changing myself from within, harnessing my own power so I could create the exact life I desired to live. Hopefully, I could inspire others along the way. I told my son my belief was that most problems continue to exist because people don't know how to use their own minds, they don't know who they really are or the power they possess.

My son talked to me about his higher goals and what he wanted to accomplish. I told him winning in life was simple but not easy and that nothing would happen overnight or without putting in work and that he would have to learn to have unwavering faith in himself if he wanted to be victorious in manifesting all of his desires. I really wanted him to understand that no matter what it looked like on the outside, and no matter what the masses were saying he was the captain of his own ship.

I was completely honest with him about the mistakes I'd made with money and being caught up trying to keep up with the Joneses'. I told him he needed to learn lessons now so he wouldn't make the same mistakes I made. I talked to him about being controlled by the big picture of the masses seeking validation, being in unhealthy relationships, and what eating poorly does to the mind.

When you don't know your true history, when you're trashing your body with unhealthy food, when you're in unhealthy relationships, when you're watching negativity, listening to negativity, and engaged in negative conversations on a regular basis it's very hard to listen to your own inner guidance.

When you're not in control of your own mind, your own thoughts, or emotions you are easy prey for the world, you are like a puppet, and the puppet master controls your narrative. I told him it took me over 30 years to learn that and I wished I would've had someone in my ear at his age giving me wisdom.

I told my son he had a lot of work to do on his attitude and mindset and that I would take him to meet the Doctah in due time so he could work through his traumatic experiences and childhood programming.

My son got emotional which was odd because he was just like me as a kid, he never cried or really showed emotions about anything.

He said, "Ma I didn't think it was possible for you to be in a situation like this. I never thought I'd see you without a car, phones getting cut off, like, really having no money staying in the house."

My son had never experienced struggling until now. Even after my divorce, money was tight, but not like this. I always had money to pay my basic bills and buy the necessities. So, I kept it real with him about how everything unraveled, and I explained the nature of being an entrepreneur and taking risks and that sometimes you win and sometimes you learn. I didn't win immediately... but I was sure as hell learning though.

I know he took heed to the information because his attitude toward me and our situation began to change. He was no longer mad. He could see the value in where we were, and we could both see how this whole mess I got into was bringing us closer together, which was the silver lining. I was happy to have his ear and I was happy we were spending quality time together, and even if he only retained a small percent of the information I was giving him, it was better than not giving it to him at all.

As I was teaching lessons to my son, I could see my own progress and how much I'd changed. My mind was different, my attitude was different, my perspective was different, my energy was different. I had a better understanding of what life was about, I was no longer taking anything personally, I could comprehend all the wisdom we have available to us in nature. I better understood all the lessons from Doctah B and the many other teachers I learned from through books. I knew who I was and what I was here to do, and I could now see in hindsight why finding oneself is the hardest thing on this earth to do.

I realized this entire journey was about unlearning everything I thought I knew and unbecoming everything I thought I was. And that the truth of who I really am at the core is no different from the truth of who we all are at the core.

We are all here for the same reason and that's to be the greatest version of ourselves. We all have a purpose but our purpose and the divine assignments we are put here to complete get buried under the big picture of the masses, our childhood programming, societal pressure, our peers, ego and our own self judgement.

We get caught up trying to be who we think we're supposed to be based on what we've seen or experienced. We pick up and perpetuate eating habits, beliefs about race, religion, relationships, education, lifestyle, career, etc. from our parents, siblings, friends, peers, teachers, TV, music, magazines, and the environment we grow up in. By the time we're 8 years old most of us are already lost, completely unaligned with who we really are.

We are never taught how to use our own minds, so we don't understand the power of our thoughts or words. We buy into a narrative that isn't really our own and we learn to use our thoughts and words as weapons against ourselves and others instead of using them to attract what we desire in life. *I* and *AM* are the two most powerful words you can use to manifest what you desire in life.

When you say **I AM**, you are speaking from the perspective of the God in you, and whatever you say after those words will manifest whether good or bad if you focus on it long enough. If you are not intentional with your thoughts, if you are not intentional with your words, you are like a tumbleweed. Life just throws you around any ole type of way and you attract things good or bad by default.

But when you're intentional with your thoughts, and intentional with your words, you can use them to shape your life, and to manifest whatever you put your mind to.

On this journey of unbecoming I learned how to be mindful of the conversations I had with myself. You know we talk to ourselves more than we talk to anyone else because we constantly have thoughts running through our minds and we are constantly processing those thoughts. When I became a witness to my own thoughts I was baffled by how many negative thoughts I had about myself on a daily basis, once I became aware of that I had to work at correcting those ANTS(Automatic Negative Thoughts) as my mentor would call them and that's where saying affirmations came in.

Affirmations were corny to me in the beginning because when I would say them it felt as if I was lying to myself, but as time went on I began believing the affirmations and I could really feel them when I said them to myself. I also found that saying them in the mirror made them feel even more impactful.

We learn to buy into so many false beliefs about ourselves, we are in a prison in our own minds because we have been programmed to believe a narrative that teaches, fear, lack, and self-hate. We only believe things like our skin is too light or dark, our hair is too nappy or too short, we aren't smart enough, or good enough because someone else told us that bullshit and we accepted it without question.

There is no such thing as being too dark, being too light, having nappy hair, or having good hair, being too short or being too tall. Your skin is beautiful if you believe it to be in your mind, no matter how light or dark you are. Your hair is beautiful, no matter the length or texture if you believe it to be. You are amazing whether you're short or tall if you believe yourself to be in your own mind.

We try to live up to what the big picture of the masses says about how we should look and what we should think about ourselves based on standards that were made up to make us feel inferior. This is where the self-hate and validation seeking creep in. If you are not aligned with your authentic self, you give society permission to control your narrative in life.

Our programming teaches us especially if you come from poverty to think from a place of fear and lack, and this mindset continues to perpetuate itself. We don't believe wealth is attainable for us, we have so many hang ups and fear-based thoughts about money when wealth and abundance is our birthright. We are programmed to believe wealth is only for a certain group of people, or that there isn't enough money in the world for us all to have more than enough, or that someone else has to lose if we desire to win in life when that's complete bull shit.

We are all supposed to be wealthy, wealth is not just about money, that's being rich and there are a lot of miserable, unfulfilled rich people in this world. Being wealthy is about having abundance in all areas of your life. An abundance of good health, abundance of love and integrity in your relationships, and an abundance of money, an abundance of peace, freedom, and joy. There is no such thing as shortage in this world there's no shortage of money, there's no shortage of good men/women to date, and there's no shortage of good health, but we are taught to buy into lackful thinking so we feel we have to compete with each other instead of supporting one another.

Again, you only believe in shortage and lack because someone told you shortage and lack existed and you accepted that bullshit with no question.

Some of us are in what seem to be hopeless circumstances but the one thing you have complete control over no matter what is your mind, and no matter where you're currently at you can begin using your mind to create an abundant life for yourself. Before anything can manifest in your reality you have to see it in your mind first.

We are taught to stay inside of our comfort zones, to follow in the footsteps of whomever we were raised by, to do what everyone else around us is doing, to be sheep, simply going through the motions each day instead of pursuing what we have passion for. We're scared to death to pursue our real dreams, a lot of people are living the lives their parents wanted for them, too afraid of breaking away from what society says they should be, too sacred to go against the grain, not brave enough to follow their own bliss.

We only have one opportunity to experience life in the physical form and everyone owes it to themselves to go after what they truly desire. We learn to settle and become complacent with mediocrity instead of pursuing our purpose. We think it's up to something or someone outside of ourselves to make real change happen in our lives.

When the reality is if you want to see a real change in your life you must change yourself from within. It was up to me and solely me to change my circumstances, no one was coming to save me, no one was going to do the work for me, and nobody owed me shit. If I desired to be, do, and have more I had to shift my way of thinking because nothing outside of you will change until you change what's going on internally.

I learned how to become very intentional with my thoughts. I would clearly write out my goals, and I lived in my imagination. Even being dead broke I would visualize myself being wealthy. Every day I pictured myself doing what I loved, making millions of dollars, being in a beautiful relationship, creating generational wealth for my family, making an impact in the world, and having ultimate freedom to do whatever I desired in life.

I also realized how hard it was for people to shift their thinking because of the level of trauma we inherit, and how much more trauma we pick up throughout life and that we never learn how to heal from it so it spreads like an infectious disease.

We have all been through different levels of trauma and you should never discount what you've been through. Yes, some people may have had it worse than you, but you owe it to yourself to heal from whatever you have been through in your life. When you heal trauma, you heal the nervous system, the emotional body and the mind.

There are different avenues to healing from trauma. For me, healing started with me prioritizing my self-care. Eating healthy and exercising regularly were two things I was in complete control of. No matter who you are or where you're at you can control what you put in your mouth, and you can control when you exercise your body. From there I was compelled to take better care of my mental and spiritual health through reading, meditation, spending time in nature, and working with Doctah B. Working with someone who not only looked like me, but could also relate to what I'd been through in life was extremely helpful in my journey of unbecoming, healing, and finding my authentic self.

When you do not heal from trauma, you are not in alignment with your authentic self and it's very hard to control your mind, shift your thinking, and create a new narrative for your life. I was so out of alignment before seeking validation, doing things to alter my body, working in low vibrational toxic environments, judging others, and trying to live up to ridiculous standards.

I was so grateful to be free from this trend of being fake, allowing my life to be controlled by a narrative that did not belong to me, buying into societal pressure, and seeking things outside of myself for validation.

That's when it clicked! My mind, body, and spirit were really free! Free from fear of being myself, free from trying to conform to the crowd, free from judgment of others, free from judgement of myself, free from every label and title I ever allowed society to attach to my being. My journey of Un-Becoming was almost complete. I was no longer on the ground in survival mode oblivious as to who I really was...
I knew I had wings

***

"'How does one become a butterfly?' she asked? You must want to fly so much that you are willing to give up being a caterpillar."- Trina Paulus

Just as only 10% of caterpillars go through the transformation of turning into butterflies only a small percentage of people are willing to go through the journey of un-becoming. They never find their authentic self, so they leave this earth never knowing their true greatness or how beautiful life is when you are living in your truth and being the highest version of yourself.

I've always been enamored with butterflies. Hell, I got one tattooed on my back one drunken night in Miami when I was in my early twenties. I didn't understand then how much my life would parallel with that of my favorite creature.

The Monarch butterfly may be the most majestic, mythological, mysterious creature on this earth. I truly believe they were put here as a mirror for us. The monarch butterfly brings the feeling of joy, freedom, and happiness when you are blessed with its presence. As it flies high in the sky, light as a feather, and as free as can be with its auburn orange wings, bordered with black and sprinkled with tiny white dots, it has a special energy. You know you're looking at a creature that went through a great deal of darkness and change in order to become what it was meant to be.

The Monarch butterfly goes through a metamorphosis that is as close to magic as we may see in real life.

Our journey to un-become everything we thought we were so we can be the best versions of ourselves is no different from the journey of the monarch butterfly.

Just as every single caterpillar has an inherent destiny to become a beautiful butterfly, we all have inherent greatness within and a purpose to fulfill on this earth. We all have gifts that are innately ours. We come into the world with gifts that can't be taken away because they are ingrained in the fiber of our very being.

We all have a different path based on our unique gifts, but each path leads to the same destination: love, peace, harmony, health, abundance, compassion, fulfilment, and happiness.

For most of our lives we are so distracted by our egos and trying to conform to the big picture of the masses. We keep ourselves in a mental prison, afraid to dig deeper into ourselves. We don't want to feel too much, we are afraid to go against the status quo, we don't question anything, we are terrified of stepping outside of what feels comfortable even if what we are comfortable with is toxic and dysfunctional. We talk ourselves out of pursuing our higher goals, we go against our intuitions, we don't trust ourselves, we settle for less than what we deserve, we judge and criticize others, we judge and criticize ourselves even worse than we criticize and judge others. Then, we use material possessions to validate ourselves and make up for the internal inadequacies we are too afraid to face.

The butterfly moves differently than the caterpillar. The butterfly is free, soaring high, and the caterpillar is on the ground surviving, trying not to get stepped on. The caterpillar brings about a different energy. You don't feel joy, peace, and happiness when you see a caterpillar as you do when you see a butterfly. The caterpillar only eats milkweed, so its flesh is very bitter. The butterfly, on the other hand, eats the sweet nectar of beautiful flowers. And you know what they say: you are what you eat!

The butterfly is free to go anywhere in the world it desires to go, and the caterpillar is restricted to the ground. The butterfly migrates to spend time with other butterflies, the caterpillar is on the ground surviving with everything else on the ground trying not to get squashed.

I spent my entire on the life on the ground in survival mode, trying to keep up with the demands of society, getting myself into toxic situations, sacrificing my own health and well-being, settling for less than I deserved, clueless as to who I was and what my purpose was, using materialism to validate my existence, surrounding myself with toxic people who were not interested in elevating in life, stuck in my comfort zone until my higher self demanded more of me.

That night in my bathroom when I broke down and asked for guidance and clarity, I had no idea what was in store. I didn't know it then but the voice that came and woke me up in the middle of night saying Now Is Time was my voice, it didn't sound like me then because it was the voice of a version of myself I didn't yet know….

That following morning I had a choice to either roll over and continue living life as the small, unfulfilled, unaware version of me or I could follow my gut instinct and do what my inner being directed me to do so I could be more.

I often tell people when they ask how I got into health and wellness that I did not choose this lifestyle it chose me, it saved me, it woke me up, it turned the lights on for me, and it compelled me to go deeper within myself.

So now that I'd gone through the dark night of the soul, did the hard inner work, faced my biggest demons, and actually changed not on the surface but changed deep within the depths of my soul everything was different.

I was moving differently, I could feel the difference in my energy, I could feel my own power, and I had a new sense of freedom about myself. I could feel the difference in how people approached, reacted, and responded to me. I could tell my energy was much different by the kind of people I was attracting into my experience.

The energy I got from others was so pleasant because I was putting good energy out into the universe. I was no longer attracted to the same people, places or things. I wasn't passing judgement on anyone else, but you can only attract from where you're vibrating at, so I was only interested in being around people on the same vibrational frequency as me. I was attracted to people who were about positivity, love, forward movement, innovation, wealth, self-ownership, elevation, and making an impact.

I was at a place of complete peace in my life. I had zero drama, I didn't dislike anyone, I wasn't angry at anyone, I didn't hate anyone, I wasn't pointing fingers at anyone, and I wasn't blaming anyone. It's impossible to keep your vibration high if you are harnessing negativity towards anyone or anything.

I was no longer trying to conform; I was totally okay with being me regardless of what anyone else thought. I was ok with being different, I was ok with people not understanding me, I was ok with people not liking me, I was ok with people saying you've changed. When people would say that to me, I would say thank you, I took it as a compliment.

Our very nature in life is to change, it's ironically amazing how badly other people want to see you stay the same though. What's more amazing than that is how fast you begin attracting what you desire when you're in alignment with who you are.

After really fully understanding the mental, physical, and spiritual metamorphosis I went through, fully embracing who I was at the core, and understanding my own energy, things I spoke into the universe began manifesting without me having to do much at all.

24

∞
_____

Attract It... Don't Chase It

Since I was a young kid, I always had an abundant mind, I always knew I wanted to have my own business, and I always knew I wanted to have a lot of money. I told myself since the age of 8 that I would become a millionaire by a certain age and I never lost sight of that goal.

After my divorce I wrote myself a letter manifesting my first million, and I had a check I wrote to myself for a million dollars taped to my nightstand. I didn't know the exact plan on how I was going to get the first million, I just knew I would get it.

Throughout this entire journey one of the biggest lessons I learned was about energy. Before, I didn't understand how much of an effect other people's energy had on me. We tell our kids that birds of a feather flock together, so make sure you surround yourself with people who are doing the right thing. Then we forget to take that same advice ourselves.

You tend to be like the people you spend the most time with, and the one thing I learned from being an entrepreneur, working with high level coaches, joining masterminds, and reading books is that wealth minded people spend time with other wealth minded people.

I loved my family and friends. It wasn't anything against them but I knew I needed to increase my circle of influence if I really desired to become a millionaire I needed to have millionaires and people on the same vibrational frequency as me in my inner circle that I knew on a personal level that I could talk to about business, money, investing and life so I put that out into the universe.

I got back focused on my digital consulting business, I had a lot more confidence in my abilities. I knew I had valuable information to share about digital business, I knew how hard I'd worked and how much I'd invested to gain the level of expertise I had, and I was no longer afraid to charge my worth.

I began attracting high end clients who had no problem paying my price. Within weeks of putting together a new digital course offer I made more money than I'd made the prior 6 months combined. I felt alive, I was super excited about business consulting just as I'd been when I first became a health coach. I loved health coaching, but business consulting gave me a different type of satisfaction. This was where I really felt my zone of genius was at when it came to my analytical mind, helping people monetize their expertise and use technology to make more money gave me a thrill I'd never felt before.

One day my cousin was on the phone with a childhood friend. When he got off the call, he told me he thought this was someone he should connect with.

"I think he's into the digital stuff like you are," he said. My cousin sent me his social media info and said, "Check him out he's doing some big things."

I later found out the friend was Uchendi Nwani, also known as the millionaire barber.

Our first conversation lasted for about 3 hours. We literally talked nonstop about digital marketing, ecommerce, digital products, different software and tools, and different business ventures. He was so open about everything, he gave me so much advice, so much insight, and we bounced so many good ideas off each other.

I got off the phone like, "Wow did I just have a 3-hour conversation with a multimillionaire in the same line of work as me?" I didn't even have to leave the house to make this connection.

Me and the millionaire barber talked regularly. He became a good friend, and we ended up working on a few ventures together.

Things were coming together. I was still underwater financially, but I could come up and breathe a little bit. More importantly, I had a blueprint, a plan, and I knew how attainable my goals were.

Throughout my journey of un-becoming there was one thing I struggled with big time, and that was my love for smoking weed. I don't know why, but a part of me had so much shame, like, I'd bought into the stigma of marijuana being bad, and a few times I tried to force myself to stop. I knew it was something I loved doing. I didn't really want to stop. I knew how much it helped me when it came to stress, anxiety, and insomnia. So, I began doing research on cannabis and quickly became obsessed with learning everything I could about this amazing plant.

I learned about the history of cannabis and how our ancestors used it from the beginning of time as medicine to heal from ailments such as inflammation, malaria, and rheumatism, and that it was used during childbirth for pain relief. Once I learned the real reasons behind cannabis being outlawed and why marijuana was considered a Schedule 1 drug and had such a negative stigma was to imprison black and brown men. I felt I had to use my face, my voice, and my influence to speak out about not only my cannabis use but also about the health benefits correlated with regular cannabis consumption to break the stigma.

Cannabis is a natural herb and a form of natural medicine, so it tied in perfectly with everything I did in the health coaching space. Plus, I saw a lot of gaps in the cannabis industry when it came to education so I knew I could use my skills as a digital creator to position myself as an influencer in the cannabis industry.

This would be a completely new venture but I felt good about it because I could combine everything I loved doing, which was educating others about health and wellness and the importance of self-care, creating and consulting about digital products, while unapologetically enjoying cannabis.

For months and months, I did research. I saw so many areas in which I could use my skills as a health coach and my expertise as a digital business consultant in the cannabis industry and it was very exciting. More than anything I felt more authentic than I ever had before. It was like pivoting into this industry was helping me step all the way into my power as a woman.

My approach to learning about the cannabis industry was the same as my approach to learning about holistic health. I watched everything I could on Netflix, Hulu, and YouTube.

I was watching a show on YouTube one day and one of the episodes was about one of the largest black-owned cannabis companies. What was so divinely crazy about this company was that my ex knew one of the CEO's and had done some work for them early on when they first started the company. So, I was familiar with the brand and used to rock their apparel but never knew the backstory. After watching the episode, I did more research and learned they were amongst the best when it came to the quality of their product. I said to myself that if I am going to position myself in this industry, I only want to be aligned with the best. I knew I could bring value to anyone I connected with in the cannabis industry so my desire was to have a meeting with the CEO's to discuss how we could synergistically work together. I put it out to the universe to make it happen when the time is right, and I left it at that.

Within a few months, I had a 5-hour sit down with both founders.

I continued using my mind to manifest desirable connections. I made countless connections right from my phone and laptop without having to leave the house. It was amazing to witness myself attracting exactly what I said I desired to attract. Not only did I have the millionaire barber, I now had millionaires in other industries too — real estate investors, attorneys, cannabis growers, and digital marketers —that I could personally connect with. I was beyond grateful.

It was crazy to think that just a few months prior, other than people in my online coaching group, I didn't know one single millionaire personally that I could call on the phone to discuss business with, and none of those in my coaching group were of color. Now I knew more than one millionaire, personally, and they were the same color as me.

I also learned that no matter how much inner work you do, how good your energy is, or how much you evolve, life will still throw curve balls your way. You will still be faced with challenges, you will still be tested, you will have to deal with unfortunate circumstances. This is inevitable, but you're mentally, physically, and spiritually equipped to handle difficulties in a much better way.

My mentor would always say, "You face the most opposition when you're about to take off. Think about a rocket, or bow and arrow, and the pull backward before the big release."

I knew the hardest part of my journey was over and that all I had to do was remember I was the captain of my own ship, in complete control of my mind.

I often felt as if I was being tested by the universe, like the universe was throwing curve balls at me purposely just to see if I'd really evolved and learned the lessons I needed to learn.

It seemed as if every curve ball was related to money and men too. Go figure, right?

Once I was out of my phase of solitude, back on social media, and getting out more, I had men from my past coming out of the woodwork like I was a dog in heat or something. After being celibate for over a year and a half, I will say I was tempted ...*very* tempted... a time or two, but I knew I had no desire to be with anyone from my past. It wouldn't be worth it so I harnessed my energy elsewhere.

I also encountered a situation or two dealing with dishonest men who lacked integrity when it came to business. I lost a significant amount of money in two deals but instead of going loco like the old me would have, I was totally unbothered. I took the experiences as valuable lessons learned.

When it came to money it was as if I just could not get ahead. No matter how much money I made in my consulting business, I kept hitting roadblocks. It was an uphill battle with me and money, for real, I swear.

The setbacks with money were so frequent it was almost comical. Every time I made a significant amount of money something would come up. I would have to remind myself this was a test, and I was going to pass it, I had to just keep my mind right. Nothing was going to break me down mentally, nothing was going to break me down spiritually, nothing was going to break me down physically. I just kept rolling with the punches because overall I knew everything I was experiencing was happening *for* me and not *to* me.

I was online one day reading about my life path number. I read something that said because you have this life path number you will experience more difficulties than most, it will feel unfair at times. As I read it, I thought to myself, *well damn.* I also knew I was mentally strong enough to handle anything that came my way.

My life path number is 1. Those on the 1 path tend to be trailblazers and visionaries who do not follow the beaten path. Those on the 1 path tend to have this innovative maverick-like mentality, they normally face more opposition than most as they navigate through life fulfilling their purposes.

Something else I enjoyed was researching the backstory of other people who shared the same life path number as me. I found so many historical people who had the same life path number as me and I found tremendous comfort and motivation in knowing their stories.

Maya Angelou, Martin Luther King, Eartha Kitt, Lebron James, Nipsey Hussle, TD Jakes, Steve Jobs, Nikola Tesla, and Walt Disney were the life path 1 names that stood out to me most. Each person went through a tremendous amount of struggle and opposition as they were fulfilling their purposes, but I looked at the impact they all made and said if I must face opposition and deal with setbacks, so be it. If I can be as purpose driven and impactful in my way as those I named before, it's worth it.

My son, on the other hand, was getting restless. He was in and out of being okay with where we were and not being okay, which was understandable. I didn't expect his mind to be as evolved as mine, so I had to have an honest conversation with him.

I told him, "Every time I've prepared to get a new car and place, I hit a major roadblock. Something in my gut is saying, 'maybe we need to stay where we are just a little longer.'"

I felt there was something I was supposed to do, and I needed to be where I was to do it. I didn't know what that something was, but I thought back to a conversation I had with my mentor before moving in with my cousin.

He said, "You're going to do something really special while you're there, this is all part of the bigger plan."

Earlier in the year I'd been invited to speak to a group of elementary students about entrepreneurship. After the response I got from the presentation I decided to come up with a program about digital entrepreneurship and my goal was to pitch this program to K-12 schools and organizations that served at risk youth, and men and women returning home from prison.

An old classmate from high school got me connected with a few directors on the school board. I reached out to all of them via email about the digital entrepreneurship program and ended up getting a meeting with a director on the Clayton County school board, the county in which I graduated high school from.

When I got to the meeting the woman I met with happened to be my old Algebra teacher from high school. We caught up, I showed her pictures of my son — I was pregnant with him when I was in her class and she remembered too.

She loved the idea of the program and felt it was very necessary. I hadn't even mentioned my desire to pitch the program to organizations that served At-risk youth and people returning home from prison when she said, "My husband is on the board of a non-profit organization called

Men on Fire. They help men coming home from prison, this is something they would be very interested in."

She immediately connected me with all the people I needed to relate to, and I was so grateful for having met with her.

Ever since I changed my lifestyle, I had a desire to help people help themselves. First, I was all about helping people attain better health. Now that I was business consulting, my desire was to teach people how to use technology to make more money.

Having my dad live with me when he came home helped me make this realization. A lot of Black men, especially those doing the most time, are in prison for a crime related to making money. I happen to believe a lot of men and women in prison have brilliant minds but because of their childhood programming, environment, lack of knowledge, and lack of resources, they use their brilliance on the wrong end of the spectrum. They opt for criminal activity as opposed to entrepreneurial activity.

I saw how hard the struggle was for my dad when he came home. Between his health, getting back and forth to the parole board, and getting accustomed to technology, it was extremely difficult. He had me there to support him and it was still hard as hell for him.

So I thought about all of the people who come home and have no support, no one there to help them shift their mindset, to help them tap into their inner gifts, to help them use their brilliance in a positive way, or to help them learn healthier habits. I could see how the cycle of going back to prison perpetuated itself.

I was so excited about my connection with *Men on Fire.* Within a few weeks the board asked if I would come and do a presentation about the digital entrepreneurship program. During the presentation I shared my story and how my life was affected by my father going to prison, what I'd accessed since he'd been home, and why I felt there was a need to teach people with a record how to start their own businesses online.

The board gave me a standing ovation after the presentation and decided they were very interested in implementing the program.

As I was leaving, one of the board members said, "You have a really great story. Have you ever thought about writing a book?"

In so many words I said, "No I'm not interested at the time."

He asked why and I said, "Well I thought about doing children's books before and I've had writing a book on my vision board for the last 5 years. I know it's something I desire to do but I don't think I'm ready. I feel like I need to live a little more, and I need to hit a certain financial goal first."

He said, "Really, what type of financial goal?"

I said, "I'd like to make my first million before I write a book."

He said, "Listen, you are ready now, you have a great story right now. What does 'live a little longer' even mean?"

Then he told me about writing his first bestselling book, *Street Rap*. He said if he would've waited, it wouldn't have become a *New York Times* bestseller.

Then he said, "What if writing your book is the thing that will get you your first million?"

When he said that, he had my ear. He told me about his publishing company and said that if I decided to go through with writing the book, he could coach me through the process. I told him I needed to think about it. We exchanged information before I left and scheduled a time to follow up.

I thought about writing a book the whole way home. At first, I kept talking myself out of it, like, "No, I can't write a memoir. I'm too private for that, I have too many things I do not desire to share, too many people would know my personal business. I'd have to tell my son things he never knew about me." So, the thought of writing a memoir was mortifying, to say the least.

I still had my old vision board from the previous year. I didn't bother making a new one because I still had the same desires. I'd recently pulled it out of the garage and taken it upstairs to the guest room I slept in at my cousin's. I had it sitting on top of my many stacks of books on the floor and the board was leaning against the wall. I looked at my vision board every day, but on this day a few things on the board jumped out at me. I picked the board up and examined it closely.

I had books on the board in three different places and right there all lined up vertically on the board was: *$1 million, make it happen, New York Times bestselling author.* Then I looked at the digital vision board I had on Pinterest and there it was again. Books, international bestselling author... and on this board I even specified the desire to have a New York Times bestselling author as my book coach.

I realized that I did nothing on my part, other than become aligned with my true complete self and I've manifested a New York Times bestselling author offering to coach me through writing my own book. For me not to move forward with writing a memoir would be a slap in the universes' face. Thinking I needed to live more, or reach certain goals first, was my way of saying I'm really scared shitless and not feeling confident enough in myself to write a book about my life. I had to get out of my own way. I'd come too far to allow fear-based thoughts to creep in.

So, I picked up the phone and called the book coach and said, "I'm in, let's do it."

We decided we would meet via phone or in person each week until I finished the book.

At our first meeting of course, he wanted to know my full story. I let him know how skeptical I was and the lack of confidence I was feeling in sharing my story. He assured me on how powerful the story was, and on how many people would benefit from reading it. So, I shifted the focus away from myself and thought more about using my story to inspire and motivate others. Once I made that mental shift, I felt much better writing the book.

I told my son I felt writing the book was the something special Doctah B predicted I'd do while living with my cousin and going through this whole mess. I'd already started looking for a new place for us to move into. He was very excited about the news.

At first, it was very hard for me to get into writing. It was so frustrating, and much harder than I imagined it would be. There was so much to remember, and my brain was scattered all over the place. I must have started typing and deleted everything 50 times.

Finally, I went and bought 6 composition notebooks and decided writing everything down freehand would be best. With the help of my coach I was able to get into a steady flow, and for several days I wrote… and wrote… and wrote everything I could remember about my life off top.

Writing like that, having to go back and think about all my life's experiences… who I was back then versus who I was now was wild. I could really see the entire puzzle of my life and how all the pieces were finally coming together.

As I was writing I began drawing inspiration from everywhere. Nature, books I read, movies I'd seen… but the greatest source was from hip-hop. During my time in solitude I really got away from listening to hip-hop and I was just getting back into listening to it. Now, my ear for hip-hop was different, more mature. I wanted to hear real hip-hop music with a story and substance.

I remember binge-watching *Hip-Hop Evolution* on Netflix with my son one night. I felt really inspired by the pioneers of hip-hop, those who really had substance in their music and used their words to speak their truth in an inspiring and uplifting way. My desire was to do the same thing with the memoir I was writing.

Once I got into the groove of it, I really enjoyed writing. It felt like another source of therapy, so I got up and wrote every day for at least 2 hours. When I wasn't working with my consulting clients, I was writing. Most weekends were spent home writing.

I never considered myself to be a writer, but I felt like this was the something I was supposed to do. Spiritually, I felt as if this book was the special something I needed to complete before officially stepping into the next phase of my life. I felt as if the memoir would be the final hurrah with my old self, as if this book was my way of paying homage to the woman I used to be before finally laying her to rest.

Everything I ever went through in life was of value to me now because I had a story to tell. I'd been through so many trials and tribulations, faced so many challenges, and made it through so many situations that could have broken me. Most importantly, I learned lessons. I matured. I went inward and mastered myself, and I had the guts to go on the journey of unbecoming. I went through the darkest nights, stripped myself of all my "cool". I faced my demons, I freed my mind from poisonous thinking, I took control of the narrative of my life, and I got into alignment with who I was at the core: A lover, free and deep rooted at heart, with pure, positive intentions for myself and others. No one could ever use anything against me or make me feel bad about anything from my past or present because I was aware of who I was and completely confident in that.

It took me breaking my ankle, changing my lifestyle, going through divorce, isolating myself from everyone, losing all of my money, burning my business to the ground, ruining my credit, and moving in with my cousin for a few months so I could completely fall apart and go through the darkest time of life to finally peel back all of the layers so I could reveal me... the real me, and I wouldn't trade any part of my journey because my time as a caterpillar was over.

I had wings now! I was too big to occupy the small uncomfortable space where I once lived, and my light was too bright to ever dim it down for those blinded by it. I was ready mentally, physically, and spiritually for the next level of my life. I was magnetic, ready to attract all things desirable. It was time for me to soar into greater heights. I was free to go anywhere my mind desired to go, but before officially taking off I needed to express my sincere adulation for my old self before officially burying her.

So, I had a mental sit down with her. I visualized my old self. I thought of all her favorite foods, her favorite TV shows, and stores. How she used to dress, what she used to talk about, and what her view of the world was like. The first thing I wanted to do with my old self was reminisce on the good, bad, and ugly times she had.

I wanted her to know I held nothing against her. I wanted her to know she was never a victim, I wanted her to know I wasn't ashamed of her, that I didn't regret one single experience she had.

I wanted her to know she held me down and if it wasn't for her I would never have found the real me. I wanted to thank her for being so tough and guarded, always speaking her mind. I wanted to thank her for being a cold-hearted bitch with an explosive temper when she needed to be.

I thought of all the crazy shit she got into, the pain, trauma, and heartbreak she experienced. I wanted to thank her for all of the time she spent on the ground in survival mode, I wanted to commend her for being brave enough to go through the dark journey of the soul, and I wanted to let her know it was all worth it because in the end I did exactly what I was supposed to do I transformed it all into love... and a story to share.

Finally, I wanted to hug her, and give her a kiss on the forehead. I wanted her to know I would miss her, laugh about her, and think of her from time to time. But most importantly, I wanted to let her know it was time for us to go our separate ways for good. I would never be her again, but I truly loved her and admired her for everything she went through.

I also wanted her to know it was a new day now. I was fully aligned with my purpose, ready to manifest my highest desires. It was time for me to officially start my life as the woman I was truly meant to be. This memoir is my final goodbye to her.

And so, Chapter 1 of the *real* story of my life begins now. I foresee high vibrational experiences, being in the greatest love, creating generational wealth and legacy for my family, traveling the world, eating lots of good healthy food, enjoying the best cannabis, and positively impacting people everywhere I go!

Stay tuned....

PS: Remember my journey of Un-Becoming started with me making my self-care a priority. Now, I challenge you to do the same.

Make the next 30 days about your health, well-being, and self-care! Spend some quiet time alone, check in with yourself, take a break from social media, eat clean, spend time in nature, rest, exercise your body, and focus on setting and accomplishing your higher goals. You never know what may come of it!

Keba Richardson was born in Atlanta, GA.

The third of seven children, growing up in the South and coming from a big family. Keba experienced it all - the good, the bad, and the ugly. Her father was a drug lord who went to prison when she was young, and her mother was a conscious, outspoken, blunt entrepreneur turned schoolteacher.

As a young girl, Keba was very rebellious and hotheaded. She became a teen mother at just 17 years old, and eventually found her way to being an exotic dancer. After enduring her share of toxic relationships, and hitting rock bottom financially, she was forced to take a journey inward so she could find her true authentic self.

On the path to self-discovery, she began studying holistic health. Her passion and knowledge about health led to her becoming a health coach, where she primarily serviced African American women, virtually. Gaining knowledge and experience about virtual business led to her launching a very successful career as digital business consultant, helping health coaches grow their businesses online.

Keba, a self-proclaimed health nut is also a cannabis advocate. She enjoys reading, working out, spending time in nature, traveling, eating good food, and listening to great music. Keba now resides in Atlanta, Ga with her teenaged son.

Keep up with Keba on her vibrant social media accounts below.

Website: Kebarichardson.com

Pretty Women Love Cannabis site coming soon!

Instagram: Keba_Richardson
Prettywomenlovecannabis_
Sexyslimselfcare30day

Facebook: Keba Richardson

LinkedIn: Keba Richardson

Pinterest: Pretty Women Love Cannabis

YouTube: Pretty Women Love Cannabis

Twitter: Pwlovecannabis

The Journey of Unbecoming